MARY
EDWARDS
WALKER

THE AMERICAN HEROES SERIES

Amelia Earhart: The Sky's No Limit by Lori Van Pelt
Chief Joseph: Guardian of the People by Candy Moulton
John Muir: Magnificent Tramp by Rod Miller
Mary Edwards Walker: Above and Beyond by Dale L. Walker

FORTHCOMING

David Crockett: Hero of the Common Man
by William Groneman III
George Washington: First in War, First in Peace
by James A. Crutchfield

Dale L. Walker, General Editor

MARY EDWARDS WALKER

Above and Beyond

DALE L. WALKER

A Tom Doherty Associates Book
New York

Frontispiece photograph courtesy of Nancy Ravas
Book design by Michael Collica

A Forge Book
Published by Tom Doherty Associates, LLC
175 Fifth Avenue
New York, NY 10010

www.tor.com

Forge® is a registered trademark of
Tom Doherty Associates, LLC.

Library of Congress Cataloging-in-Publication Data

Walker, Dale L.
    Mary Edwards Walker : above and beyond / Dale L. Walker.—
1st hdbk. ed.
        p. cm.
    Includes bibliographical references (p. 209) and index (p. 213).
    ISBN 0-765-31065-1
    EAN 978-0765-31065-1
    1. Walker, Mary Edwards, 1832–1919.   2. Women physicians—United
States—Biography.   3. United States—History—Civil War, 1861–1865—
Women.   4. United States—History—Civil War, 1861–1865—Medical
care.   I. Title.
    R154.W18W35 2005
    610'.82'092—dc22

                                                    2004030227

First Edition: June 2005

PRINTED IN THE UNITED STATES OF AMERICA

0   9   8   7   6   5   4   3   2   1

To some other great Walkers
Alice McCord
Dianne Laurie
Eric Paul
Christopher Dale
Michael Scott
John Randall

"It is the times which are behind *me*."

—Mary Edwards Walker, M.D.

"She lived a life of determined unconventionality . . ."

—Secretary of War Edwin M. Stanton

"I would rather have that Medal than be
President of the United States."

—President Harry Truman

Contents

Contents

Contents

Preface

For such a combative, opinionated woman—one who knew instinctively that she had a niche in history—Mary Edwards Walker left only a fragmentary record of her life. Where it is most needed, her "voice" is missing.

An example of this is her silence on so many of her contemporaries, many of them celebrated figures in Mary's own lifetime, many with whom she shared war experiences or stages in women's rights meetings. Nor do we have her voice—her *attitude*—except for a few scattered exceptions, on the great national and international issues of her long life.

She was a Civil War veteran, an eyewitness to many of the horrors of America's bloodiest war, but while hating what she saw, she believed strongly in the preservation of the Union and presumably (she never really said one way or the other) believed the war inevitable and necessary. She remained intensely patriotic to the end of her days, but left only a few random remarks on the two wars she saw from the sidelines.

Of the Spanish-American War of 1898, she was quoted as being opposed to the expansionism in the Philippines, later made some cruel remarks about President McKinley, and had nothing good to say about Theodore Roosevelt. She was opposed to the United States joining England, France, and other allies in World War I, and had disdain for President Wilson for involving the nation in the conflict. Otherwise, the slate is blank.

Mary devoted a few lines in her autobiographical fragment, "Incidents Connected with the Army," to meeting Dorothea Dix at the Indiana Hospital in Washington early in the war, but of so many other contemporaries said nothing. Even of her comrades in the women's rights revolution she left little or no notice. She rarely mentioned Elizabeth Cady Stanton, Mary Ashton Rice Livermore, Lucy Stone, Belva Ann Lockwood, or Amelia Jenks Bloomer, and left no words about Clara Barton, Victoria Woodhull, Frederick Douglass (with whom she once marched in a suffrage rally), or on the many luminous figures she met and came to know.

At the source of the problem, I believe, is that Mary Walker found writing difficult, had no flair for it, and so avoided it. What we have of her authorship—her small, self-published books, her "Incidents" manuscript, scraps from her columns in the women's periodical *Sybil*—shows the haste and labor behind its creation.

She admitted she could never manage to abide by her father's advice that she keep a daily journal, and that presents to the modern writer the predicament of resolving such problems as the countless gaps—some of them months long—in the record of her life. For this reason, when it seemed necessary, I have had to speculate and make use of such equivocations as "perhaps," "probably," and "more than likely."

Even so, *Mary Edwards Walker: Above and Beyond* is a work of nonfiction. I have invented nothing in it. I wish she had left more of her own words to work with, but piecing together her story from her own scattered works, the memories of those who knew her, newspaper reports, and from the pioneer researchers named in the sources in this book proves that Mary Walker's extraordinary and heroic life requires no invention.

DALE L. WALKER
June 1, 2004

MARY
EDWARDS
WALKER

Prologue

I n Oswego, New York, on June 10, 1982, the United States Postal Service issued a twenty-cent stamp commemorating "Dr. Mary Walker, Army Surgeon." Under the benevolent likeness of Dr. Walker, looking very much like a demure character from a Louisa May Alcott novel, was the legend "Medal of Honor."

The stamp must have puzzled those who missed the Postal Service publicity announcing its issue. A *woman* won the Medal of Honor? Who was Dr. Mary Walker? What extraordinary act, above and beyond the call of duty, in what conflict with what enemy, had earned her the nation's highest tribute for military valor?

Among the facts about "Dr. Mary Walker, Army Surgeon," missing from the stamp announcement were these:

—She was an indefatigable foe of traditional female dress, male domination, and wedding vows, and preached women's rights in an era when nobody wanted to hear about them.

—She was a physician with startling ideas, among them that battlefield surgeons were amputating limbs too indiscriminately, and that common medical practices such as bleeding, blistering, and heavy doses of mercuric compounds were foolhardy.

—During the Civil War, while she was never actually in the army and never an "Army Surgeon," she doctored, nursed, and counseled wounded, maimed, and dying soldiers; ministered to suffering civilians on both the North and South sides of the conflict; and spent four months in a hellhole of a Confederate prison.

To the men who ran Congress, to the functionaries of the government bureaus in Washington, Mary Walker, their frequent visitor and eternal correspondent, was a cantankerous, abrasive, harassing, professional scold who was perhaps insane; but to those who saw her tiny figure hovering over their bloody pallets in battlefield hospital tents, she was an angel of mercy.

Her tendency to attract such divided opinions resurfaced in 1977 when her name was restored on the roll of Medal of Honor recipients, and again in 1982 when the postage stamp honoring her was unveiled in her hometown of Oswego. In those years, military periodicals carried letters and articles by old-school soldiers expressing doubt that Mary Walker's service in the Civil War actually warranted the medal.

She was not easy to know or understand in her own time (even her female contemporaries, stumping for the right to vote, for temperance, and for similar issues, often found her more of an embarrassment than a comrade at the barricades) and she is much more difficult to know and understand today, eighty-six years after her death.

Two things about her are certain: She was a child of the Victorian age who abided by some of its mores but defied most of them; and, there is more to her life that is heroic than the deeds that earned her the Medal of Honor.

★ ★ ★ ★ ★ ★ **1** ★ ★ ★ ★ ★ ★ ★

Bunker Hill Farm

1

Long before the first white settlers arrived in Oswego, New York, on the eastern shore of Lake Ontario, in the mid-1600s, the Iroquois people had given it its name, a word meaning "pouring out place," referring to the point where the Oswego River emptied into the big lake. The settlers who broke the ground and built their homesteads along the river were followed by the ancient triumvirate of advancing civilization: Trade, Cross, and Flag. In 1775, fur traders made Oswego a port of call; missionaries came, seeking to Christianize the Indians; and British redcoats followed, building two forts at the mouth of the river and maintaining control of the strategic area three hundred miles northwest of New York City until 1796.

In the first half of the nineteenth century, with the river crowded with packet boat and similar seagoing traffic, its shores bedecked with grain elevators and flour mills, the town boomed. Construction of the Oswego Canal, linking the Erie Canal with Lake Ontario, resulted in a heavy traffic transporting salt from Syracuse, grain from the Midwest, and all manner of products in and out of the tiny settlement. An inventive gentleman named Thomas Kingsford added a significant chapter to Oswego's development when he devised a method to extract starch from corn and built the world's largest starch factory in the town in 1848.*

2

Oswego had a population of about three thousand when Mary Edwards Walker was born there on November 26, 1832, the fifth child of Alvah Walker and Vesta Whitcomb, who farmed a thirty-three-acre tract off Bunker Hill Road.

Of Vesta Whitcomb Walker we know little except that she was a native of Greenwich, Massachusetts, born there in 1801, and traced her heritage from a long line of New Englanders. In a family connection of special interest in Mary Walker's story, Vesta was a cousin of Robert Green Ingersoll, the celebrated nineteenth-century lawyer, orator, and agnostic.

He is worth noting further for he was a public figure, prominent in newspaper columns for his liberal views on religion, literature, and politics. Vesta certainly would have followed his controversial career and spoke of him, her famous cousin, in the Walker household. Ingersoll may have even paid the Walkers a visit in the course of his New York speaking engagements.

Born in 1833, thus more than thirty years younger than Vesta Walker, Ingersoll came from Dresden, New York, on the

---

* Today, the old Town of Oswego (population about eight thousand), where Mary Walker was born, lies just west of the City of Oswego (pop. twenty thousand).

shore of Seneca Lake, the son of a Congregational minister and fiery abolitionist. Robert rose to eminence as a lawyer in Illinois and later in Washington, and as a Civil War veteran known for his electrifying speeches on behalf of the party of Abraham Lincoln. From the end of the war to his death in 1899, in an era when oratory was a dominant form of entertainment (as Mary Walker would soon learn), Ingersoll became America's most eloquent public speaker, nonconformist thinker, and agnostic. A tall, high-domed, handsome figure, called "Royal Bob" by his admirers, he was a beloved friend of Elizabeth Cady Stanton and other pioneers of the women's movement, and spoke movingly of the importance of family and the virtues of hearth and home. He thrived on theological controversy—he praised the Bible as literature but was a confirmed antireligionist, especially critical of fundamentalist Christianity—and to many among the religious orthodoxy he represented all the evils of atheism.

If he visited his cousin Vesta in the Walker home after the Civil War, he would have shared his war stories and progressive ideas with Mary and her parents, especially her freethinking father.

3

Alvah Walker, who traced his ancestry to a Plymouth Colony settler who came to America in 1643, was born in Greenwich, Massachusetts, in 1798. An itinerant carpenter as a young man, he traveled and worked framing and shingling houses in New York State, Pittsburgh, Boston, Kentucky, Mississippi, and Louisiana. By 1821, according to the pioneering research into Walker's youth by Professor Charles M. Snyder, Alvah visited the New Orleans battlefield where Andrew Jackson defeated the British six years before, and saw cannonball marks on trees and the unearthed bones of the combatants.

Mary, when she made a brief attempt to compose an autobiography after the Civil War, added a bit to the Walker family history, writing,

> My great-grandfather, who was in the army long before the Revolutionary War and whose name is on the Record of the State of Massachusetts as Jessie Snow of Hardwich, Mass., kept a daily journal, portions of which, with the date on nearly every page, is still in existence. He was also a Revolutionary soldier and suffered the hardships of those trying times.

Jessie Snow's daily journal-keeping was a habit Alvah Walker emulated, Mary said, keeping such a daily record from about the age of ten and continuing it "up to the time of his death which was upon his eighty-second birthday." He urged all his children to keep such a record and Mary did so sporadically, to improve her writing, but, as she wrote later, neither she nor her sisters "kept up their daily journal for any great length of time."

Alvah Walker was about twenty-four when he returned from his travels to Boston and there met twenty-year-old Vesta Whitcomb. They married in 1822 and settled first in Syracuse where he worked at his carpentry and apparently also became attracted to farming. During the decade they lived in the Syracuse area, the Walker family grew to six with the birth of four daughters, all given vaguely Latin, celestial, names: Vesta (born in 1823), Aurora (1825), Luna (1827), and Cynthia (1828). The fifth child, Mary Edwards (1832)—the middle name honoring a Walker aunt in Massachusetts—was born shortly after Alvah sold their Syracuse home and settled on the Bunker Hill farmland in Oswego. There, too, in 1833, a son, Alvah Jr., was born.

Father Walker was intelligent and industrious. He cleared the Bunker Hill land and built a home, barn, and the town's first schoolhouse on the property. Later, when the Oswego district opened a school, he converted his to a "mechanic's shop" where he made doors, sashes, coffins, and whatever cabinetry work came his way, and served as general handyman to his neighbors. With a family of eight to support, Alvah was never able to pay off the mortgage on the farm but the family prospered intellectually if not economically. He read up on medicine, became a self-taught country doctor, an outspoken foe of liquor and tobacco, a churchgoing Christian who claimed to have read the entire Bible six times yet remained free of dogmatic ideas. He was curious, studied the heavens and nature, followed the news, tinkered, fixed, and invented.

Like his grandfather Snow, Alvah kept a daily journal but filled it with mundane notices of work done: "Trim apple tree"; "Chop wood"; "Skinned a calf "; "Fix the well"; "Cleaned cistern," "72 years old, went to city got a file, kerosene"; "Went to hear a Mormon preach, twice"; "Read the Tribune"; "My mare had a foal today." He scarcely mentioned his family, nor did he record his ideas, impressions of the news he read, least of all his innermost thoughts.

A steadfast Yankee abolitionist, his farm served as a "station" in the Underground Railroad system that assisted southern slaves to freedom—many of whom were conveyed to western New York and into Canada. And, perhaps because of the influence of his forebears, Alvah's education (about which nothing is known), as well as his naturally curious and inventive nature, some of his ideas were those of a freethinker. In the nineteenth century, this was synonymous with skeptic and, as with Robert Ingersoll, agnostic, but in Alvah's case, it signified independence of mind and what came to be called progressive.

One of his many egalitarian ideas had a lifelong effect on his fifth child. Since all the daughters were expected to perform a man's work on the farm, he forbade them to wear corsets or any tight-fitting clothing, believing such garments impeded the circulation of the blood.

4

Mary's education began among the books in her father's farmhouse and in the one-room school conducted by Alvah, Vesta, and the older sisters on the family farm. There is also a vague reference to her attending a nearby seminary where she received instruction in mathematics, philosophy, grammar, and hygiene—enough education in all so that in 1852 she was hired to teach school in the village of Minetto, five miles south of Oswego.

While her sisters were content to teach, and her brother Alvah Jr., to farm (and perform as magician and ventriloquist in regional puppet shows), Mary had other plans. She had pored over her father's medical texts, watched him "doctor" sick and injured farmhands, even assisted him in his primitive farmhouse medical practice, and was determined to save her minuscule teacher's salary and find a place to study medicine.

Blackwell

1

By some peculiar geographical harmony, the remote hamlet of Oswego lay just over fifty miles northeast of two other obscure New York towns—Geneva and Seneca Falls—each to make an indelible mark on American history and each to become consequential in Mary Walker's life.

The agricultural settlement of Geneva, located at the tip of Seneca Lake in west-central New York and incorporated in 1806, was certainly known to Alvah and Vesta Walker, and subsequently to Mary. The town's Geneva Medical College opened in 1834 as the thirtieth medical school founded in North America and the seventh in New York, and in 1849 graduated, by accident, the first female physician in the United States. Whether Mary investigated Geneva College or attempted to enroll there is unknown, but when she made up her mind to study medicine she knew of the woman who, just six years before, had paved the way for her to do so.

The woman was Elizabeth Blackwell, born in 1821 in Bristol, England, who came to New York with her family in 1832, the year Mary Walker was born. The Blackwells, like the Walkers, were societal rebels. Samuel Blackwell, Elizabeth's father, made a good living as a sugar refiner but his passion lay in church and government reform and antislavery promotion. After meeting the eminent radical abolitionist William Lloyd Garrison in New York City, the slavery issue consumed Samuel to his death. The Blackwell children were all classically educated by tutors at home and in private schools in England and New York. Elizabeth's brother Henry, another feverish abolitionist, also became a tireless worker for women's suffrage; her younger sister Emily (who became the second female physician in the United States) campaigned for suffrage and other women's issues.

Samuel Blackwell's fortunes faltered soon after he arrived in America. He moved his family from New York to Jersey City, then to Cincinnati, where he died in 1838, leaving his wife Hannah and their nine children virtually penniless.

Following Samuel's sudden death, Hannah Blackwell, together with Elizabeth and her older sisters, Ana and Marian, opened a private school to support the family. The venture proved successful, mother and daughters bringing an English accent and a fine education in literature, art, music, and languages to the culture-famished frontier town of Cincinnati.

For almost a decade Elizabeth was content to teach. After she left home she found classroom work in Henderson, Kentucky, and in North and South Carolina, but at some point in her twenties decided upon a new calling. She began reading medical texts with the revolutionary idea that a female with female health problems might prefer consulting with a female physician.

At first the necessities of studying and practicing medicine repulsed her. This petite, blond, soft-spoken young woman, accustomed to a quiet, intellectual life, recoiled at thoughts of the bloody horrors of the surgical theater, of dissecting cadavers in medical classrooms, of treating the diseases and abominations of the human body that would be presented to her by her patients. But, as she said later, "The idea of winning a doctor's degree gradually assumed the aspect of a great moral struggle, and the moral fight possessed immense attraction for me." So, she saved as much of her teaching salary as she could (as would Mary Walker in the near future) and began applying for medical school admission.

After numerous rejections (from, some sources say, twenty-nine New England and northeastern schools) Blackwell's application to enter Geneva College in rural New York State was accepted—but only by accident. The professors who read her letter referred it to a group of medical students who thought the letter was a hoax, perhaps devised by a rival college, and voted to accept her. When it was discovered to be a genuine application, the students welcomed her while the professors remained wary.

2

Now twenty-six years old, Blackwell entered Geneva College's medical school in the winter of 1847 and went about her studies with fearless determination. She turned out to be unfazed by anatomy classes, the dissections of male cadavers, and even such practical experience as work in a Philadelphia almshouse where she saw the ravages of venereal disease.

She graduated at the head of her class in January 1849, receiving the first medical degree granted to a woman in the United States, but learned quickly that the degree in medicine did not translate to a medical practice, at least not for a woman. Unable to find a hospital position and seeing private practice as impossible, she sailed to France and in Paris found work at La Maternité, an old restored convent and famed "lying-in hospital"—one specializing in obstetrics. There she contracted an infection that left her blind in one eye and forced her to abandon any hope of practicing surgery—but not general medicine. She moved on to London and joined the staff of Saint Bartholomew's Hospital where her status as a female physician was as rare as in the United States. Her role had one positive effect, however, as it brought her into contact with Florence Nightingale, whose heroic work in Turkey during the Anglo-Russian War of 1854 to 1856 would establish her as the paragon of modern nursing and of women in medicine in general.

Blackwell returned to New York in 1851 but was turned away from the city's hospitals when she sought employment, and was denied lodging and office space by landlords when she attempted to set up a private practice. Her Geneva Medical College diploma, her letters of recommendation from Paris and London carried no weight: a female doctor? Unheard of.

She purchased a modest house in Manhattan and opened a medical office, treating women and children—no male patient would deign to cross her threshold. After her sister Emily, now with her own medical degree (she had been denied enrollment at Elizabeth's alma mater, Geneva Medical College), joined her, Blackwell began giving lectures on health, a collection of which she published in 1852 as *The Laws of Life; with Special Reference to the Physical Education of Girls.*

In 1853, Blackwell opened a dispensary in the tenement district of New York City. The walk-in facility, later named the New York Infirmary for Women and Children, was operated by Emily Blackwell, trained the first Civil War nurses, and remained open for forty-six years.

After a year-long lecture tour of Great Britain, Elizabeth, in 1859, again returned to the United States and resumed work at the infirmary. The Civil War interrupted her efforts to expand the clinic to include a medical college and a nursing school, but the war gave the Blackwell sisters a new mission. They helped organize the Women's Central Association of Relief, which selected and trained nurses for service in the war, a venture that led to the creation of a powerful force in the Civil War, the United States Sanitary Commission. This formidable legion of women volunteers—seven thousand local branches across the nation by 1863—badgered Congress to pass medical reform bills, raised millions of dollars (spending over $20 million on its efforts during the course of the war), opened veterans' homes, and launched its agents into the battle zones to raise the standard of the army's medical care.

3

While no evidence exists that Elizabeth Blackwell and Mary Walker actually met, their work in Washington at the outset of the war might well have provided the opportunity. Each was among the first physicians to offer their services to the Union; each worked in hospitals in the capital in the opening weeks of the war. Mary had to know of Blackwell, whose graduation from Geneva College, just fifty miles from Oswego, set a precedent that benefited all women seeking to study medicine. Blackwell may have even known of Dr. Mary E. Walker, whose eccentric dress and ideas were reported early on in the press in Washington and New York.

Both women were outspoken, although Blackwell preferred a podium and a low-key approach to her issues while Mary was at home on the stump as much as in the lecture hall, and often had a shrill message to deliver. Despite their differences, the two had shared experiences as female physicians. Blackwell's campaigns for the acceptance of women in medicine probably seemed a minor matter to Mary, but she would have cheered her colleague's work in urging women to learn more about their bodies and healthy living. And, she would have read with enthusiasm Blackwell's energetic treatises on such subjects as sex education for children, women's suffrage, hygiene, abolition of prostitution and white slavery, and morality in government.

4

Elizabeth Blackwell's precedent-setting fifteen-month experience at Geneva College, and Mary Walker's Oswego upbringing, as well as her own forthcoming medical school advent, fit perfectly into the midcentury milieu of upstate New York. The region was the national center—a "hotbed" to the conventionally minded—of such "isms" as abolitionism, spiritualism, and agnosticism, and served as a base for the temperance movement, Unitarian controversies, prison reform, and, chief among these perceived "radical" causes, the campaign for women's rights.

This latter idea was not entirely unknown to well-born, educated young women in the early years of the nineteenth century. Blackwell*—and possibly Mary Walker, through her parents' progressive ideas—was probably acquainted with the work of Margaret Fuller (1810–1850), of Cambridgeport, Massachusetts, friend of the transcendentalists Ralph Waldo Emerson, Bronson Alcott, and Henry David Thoreau. Fuller wrote for *The Dial,* Horace Greeley's *New York Tribune,* and other influential periodicals on urban poverty, social justice, prison reform, abolitionism, women's suffrage, and educational and political equality for women and minorities, all favored subjects among the liberal minded of the era.

Fuller and other reform-minded women of the midcentury were well acquainted with the beaconlike work, *A Vindication of the Rights of Women* by Mary Wollstonecraft, published in England in 1792, which called for women to resist "male domination." Wollstonecraft's ideas gave a philosophical foundation not only for the suffrage movement but for the entire campaign for sexual equality.

---

* She returned to England in 1869. At the time of her death there, in May 1910, there were 7,399 licensed female physicians and surgeons in the United States.

Seneca Falls

1

When Mary Walker was sixteen and the world's largest starch factory was under construction in her hometown, a radical idea was being debated at a gathering just a two-day buggy ride southwest of Owego. The idea—that women had certain God-given and Constitutional rights that were being denied to them—would preoccupy Mary for the rest of her life.

The event, America's first women's rights convention, opened on July 19, 1848, at Seneca Falls, New York, fifty-four miles from Oswego and thirteen miles north of Geneva. The gathering at the town's Wesleyan Methodist Church was publicized only by a small, unsigned notice in the *Seneca County Courier,* but as Lucretia Mott, one of its organizers, said, "It will be a beginning."

The assembly had its origins in London in 1840 when Mott, of Nantucket, Massachusetts, Elizabeth Cady Stanton of Johnstown, New York, and some other American abolitionists appeared at the World Anti-Slavery Convention and, being females, were refused seats. Stanton, age twenty-five and newly married, and Mott, forty-seven, a Quaker preacher and vocal veteran of reform, spoke of organizing a meeting on the suppression of women, but eight years passed before the idea reached fruition.

In the summer of 1848, Stanton and Mott met again at a social gathering in Waterloo, New York, that included several other women, all Quakers except for Stanton, and all anti-slavery and temperance champions. Among the topics of discussion at the meeting were New York's recently passed Married Women's Property Rights Act, determined to be a significant but flawed bill, as well as temperance and abolition issues. Stanton, now mother of three small children and living in nearby Seneca Falls, spoke on the need for a convention "to discuss the social, civil, and religious condition and rights of women" and to bring these issues before the public.

By the time the two-day convention opened on July 19, a sort of rural word-of-mouth telegraph and the notice in the Seneca County newspaper had spread the news and a crowd of some three hundred (including forty men) wedged into the Wesleyan Methodist Church to hear what "rights" the women were claiming. Ironically, since none of the female organizers wished to preside over the gathering, the task was undertaken by Lucretia Mott's husband, James.

Elizabeth Stanton, using the Declaration of Independence as her model, drew up the Declaration of Sentiments that defined the intent of the convention. The document stated that "all men and women are created equal" and proceeded to list eighteen "injuries and usurpations" (the same number of charges leveled against the king of England that precipitated the American Revolution) "on the part of man toward woman." She also drafted eleven resolutions asserting that women had a natural equality with men in all walks of life. Among these declarations, one was considered particularly radical: It was the duty of women to campaign for the right to vote. To this, Quaker Lucretia Mott told her collaborator, "Why, Lizzie, thee will make us ridiculous," but Stanton stood firm. "I persisted," she said, "for I saw clearly that the power to make the laws was the right through which all other rights could be secured."

At first, all the decrees except that on suffrage ("Resolved, That it is the duty of the women of this country to secure to themselves their sacred right to the elective franchise") were adopted unanimously by the conventioneers. The men in the predominantly Quaker audience commonly avoided voting and Quaker women had little interest in the franchise, but the eloquent Frederick Douglass, the former slave and current editor of the *Rochester North Star,* convinced the gathering to agree on the most controversial of the resolutions. Ultimately, all were signed by sixty-eight women and thirty-two men in attendance.

A few days after the Seneca Falls Convention Frederick Douglass wrote in his newspaper, "A discussion of the rights of animals would be regarded with far more complacency by many of what are called the wise and the good of our land, than would be a discussion of the rights of woman."

During the closing session of the conference, Lucretia Mott presented a final resolution "for the overthrowing of the monopoly of the pulpit, and for the securing to woman equal participation with men in the various trades, professions and commerce." It, too, was adopted by the one hundred women and men who signed Elizabeth Cady Stanton's Seneca Falls Declaration.

Press coverage of the convention was sparse, the few New York notices largely negative. The *Oneida Whig* of August 1, 1848, expressed outrage at the goings-on at Seneca Falls: "Was there ever such a dreadful revolt?" the *Whig* editor asked, referring to the women who would "set aside the statute, 'wives submit yourselves unto your husbands.'" He went on to call the convention "the most shocking and un-natural incident ever recorded in the history of womanity" and asked his male readers to consider the horrific consequences of such ideas: "If our ladies will insist on voting and legislating, where, gentlemen, will be our dinners and our elbows? where our domestic firesides and the holes in our stockings?"

There were a few sympathetic articles such as that in the *Auburn National Reformer,* which, on August 31, 1848, under the heading WOMEN OUT OF THEIR LATITUDE, took issue with those "breathing the most profound contempt for the rights of one half of the human race—founded on the assumption of man's great superiority." The editor opined that "present laws and customs makes the woman and 'niggers' of the country exactly on a par, so far as their rights are now respected. . . . we would ask for but one valid reason why woman should be deprived of their equal rights as an intelligent being."

Stanton, while disturbed over its sensationalism and misrepresentations, understood the value of press attention. "Just what I wanted," she said when *New York Herald* publisher James Gordon Bennett printed the entire Declaration of Sentiments, together with his own derisive sentiments. "Imagine the publicity given to our ideas by thus appearing in a widely circulated sheet like the *Herald*," she said.

Within three years of Seneca Falls, Stanton and Susan Brownell Anthony, an Adams, Massachusetts, teacher and temperance lecturer from a Quaker family, were devoting their lives to the suffrage cause and the entire women's rights movement.*

2

When Bennett's *New York Herald* published her Declaration of Sentiments soon after the Seneca Falls Convention, Elizabeth Stanton observed, "It will start women thinking, and men too; and when men and women think about a new question, the first step in progress is taken."

Alvah and Vesta Walker must have known of the gathering

---

* Mott died in 1880, Stanton in 1902, and Anthony in 1906. In 1920, when the United States Senate passed the Nineteenth Amendment, giving women the right to vote, seventy-two years after Seneca Falls, only one of the sixty-eight female signers of Stanton's Declaration survived. She was Charlotte Woodward Pierce, who had been a teenage schoolteacher and glove maker in Waterloo, New York. She was too ill to vote on election day, and died in 1921 at age ninety-two.

just over fifty miles south of their Oswego farm and would have been among those thinking sympathetically about the new question. They certainly read of the convention in the aftermath, when some New York newspapers were running ridiculing editorials and news dispatches about the event. Alvah's ideals, especially those directed toward his daughters, preceded the expressed opinions of Stanton, Mott, and the other activists at Seneca Falls, and it seems likely that Mary Walker, even at age sixteen, learned of the Declaration of Sentiments at her father's knee and embraced them then and for the rest of her life.

"We hold these truths to be self-evident," Stanton had announced, "that all men and women are created equal . . . The history of mankind is a history of repeated injuries and usurpations on the part of man toward woman . . ."

Among the usurpations:

"He has never permitted her to exercise her inalienable right to the elective franchise. . . ."

"He has taken from her all right in property, even to the wages she earns. . . ."

"He has withheld from her rights which are given to the most ignorant and degraded men—both natives and foreigners. . . . she is compelled to promise obedience to her husband, he becoming, to all intents and purposes, her master—the law giving him power to deprive her of her liberty and to administer chastisement. . . ."

"He has monopolized nearly all the profitable employments, and from those she is permitted to follow, she receives but a scanty remuneration."

The divorce laws, Stanton said, "closes against her all the avenues to wealth and distinction . . ." She asserted that women suffer under a different code of morals, men having "usurped the prerogative of Jehovah himself." This, she said, led to a lessening of a woman's self-respect and made "her willing to lead a dependent and abject life."

Since women have been "fraudulently deprived of their most sacred rights," she said, "we insist that they have immediate admission to all the rights and privileges which belong to them as citizens of the United States."

This dynamic call to action, "to uplift woman's fallen divinity upon an even pedestal with man's," proved to be Mary Walker's lifelong marching orders. She might well have had the Declaration of Sentiments tacked on her bedroom wall in the Walker family farmhouse together with Stanton's vibrant speech of July 19, 1848, in which she declared:

Now is the time for the women of this country, if they would save our free institutions, to defend the right, to buckle on the armor that can best resist the keenest weapons of the enemy—contempt and ridicule. The same religious enthusiasm that nerved Joan of Arc to her work nerves us to ours. . . .

We do not expect our path will be strewn with the flowers of popular applause, but over the thorns of bigotry and prejudice will be our way, and on our banners will beat the dark storm clouds of opposition from those who have entrenched themselves behind the stormy bulwarks of custom and authority, and who have fortified their position by every means, holy and unholy. But we will steadfastly abide the result. Unmoved we will bear it aloft. Undauntedly we will unfurl it to the gale, for we know that the storm cannot rend from it a shred, that the electric flash will but more clearly show to us the glorious words inscribed upon it, "Equality of Rights."

3

On one matter alone would Mary Walker come to disagree with Stanton's clarion call—a matter instilled in her by her progressive but practical-minded father whose four daughters were trained to work on the Walker farm like men.

In the opening session of the Seneca Falls Convention, Stanton stated, "We do not propose to petition the legislature to make our husbands just, generous, and courteous, to seat every man at the head of a cradle, and to clothe every woman in male attire. . . . the gentlemen need feel no fear of our imitating that, for we think it in violation of every principle of taste, beauty, and dignity; notwithstanding all the contempt cast upon our loose, flowing garments, we still admire the graceful folds, and consider our costume far more artistic than theirs."

Mary Walker's disavowal of this sentiment would later define her place among the "free women" of America, but one of Stanton's list of grievances against the male populace was to be quickly encountered: "He has denied her the facilities for obtaining a thorough education—all colleges being closed against her."

OTHER PIONEERS OF WOMEN'S RIGHTS

Lucy Stone (1818–1893) of West Brookfield, Massachusetts, was the daughter of a wealthy farmer and tanner. At an early age Stone took issue with the Bible's admonition to Eve, "and thy desire shall be to thy husband, and he shall rule over thee." She lectured widely as an abolitionist and on equality for women and organized the first national Women's Rights Convention, held in Worcester, Massachusetts, in 1850. She married Henry Blackwell, a crusader for women's suffrage.

Julia Ward Howe (1819–1910). Born in New York City, the daughter of wealthy banker, Howe was active in the American Anti-Slavery Society and with her husband, Samuel Gridley Howe, edited the abolitionist journal *Commonwealth*. Also involved in the world peace and suffrage movements, she became the first woman to be elected to American Academy of the Arts (1890). A poet and friend of Longfellow's, Howe published her "Battle Hymn of the Republic" in *The*

Atlantic Monthly in 1862 and was paid five dollars for it.

Mary Ashton Rice Livermore (1820–1905). A deeply religious Bostonian married to a minister, Livermore tutored on a Virginia plantation in 1839 and became a strong abolitionist and factory workers' advocate. A staunch Republican, she campaigned for Abraham Lincoln and undertook relief work during the Civil War. She organized the Chicago Women Suffrage Convention, which met in 1869, was active in the Women's Christian Temperance Union, became editor of the women's rights journal *The Agitator*, and with Lucy Stone and Julia Ward Howe coedited *The Women's Journal*.

Belva A. Lockwood (1830–1917) was born in Royalton, New York, graduated from Genesee College (later Syracuse University) in 1857, and moved to Washington, D.C., where she opened a school. Married to the Reverend Ezekiel Lockwood, she began studying law in 1868 but was refused admission to several law schools because of her sex. She managed to study law at the National University Law School in Washington, D.C., from which she graduated but was able to receive her diploma only after she appealed to the school's president, Ulysses S. Grant. In 1879, Lockwood had the honor of becoming the first woman admitted to the bar of the United States Supreme Court. She was a suffragette and a dedicated world peace and women's rights worker.

Amelia Jenks Bloomer (1818–1894), born in Homer, New York, and married to a Quaker reformer, became a temperance and suffrage lecturer, and an advocate of marriage-law reform and higher education for women. She attended but was not an active participant in the Seneca Falls Convention of 1848. An early champion of dress reform for women, she favored a bodice and full pantaloons reaching to the ankle, over which a short skirt reached just below the knee—in other words a jacket and slacks under a short skirt. The slacks became widely known as "bloomers." Many women's rights activists experimented with the outfit, including Susan

B. Anthony and Elizabeth Cady Stanton, but most—including Bloomer herself, but with the notable exception of Mary Walker—eventually abandoned it because of the ridicule it elicited that was seen as undermining more important social reforms.

Medicine

1

Mary Walker determined, at age twenty-one, to seek a career in medicine. Whether she was inspired by assisting in her father's homemade medical practice and poring over his texts, or by Elizabeth Blackwell's example at Geneva College, or some mixture of the two, there is no precise record. It is safe to guess that she applied to several medical schools, probably Geneva among them (which, after graduating Elizabeth Blackwell in 1849 did not admit women for several years), before gaining admission to the Syracuse Medical College in December 1853.

She had saved her teaching money and may have had some help from her father to pay the tuition: fifty-five dollars for each of three thirteen-week terms leading to a medical degree. And, since Syracuse lay thirty-five miles southeast of Oswego, she would have had to live in a dormitory, her room and board costing $1.50 per week.

The college, only two years old, was composed of a nine-member faculty that conducted its classes. When Mary enrolled there, it was distinguished in admitting women (three had been admitted in 1849, the year Elizabeth Blackwell graduated from Geneva College) and in its approach to teaching medicine.

At the time she began her studies—a time when phrenology, spiritualism, and mesmerisms were considered sciences—medicine was a dubious, low-paying profession. It was clogged with primitive folkways and a bewildering and contentious array of techniques to treat disease, most of them specious, many dangerous, all vying for "scientific" recognition. (In her era, as Charles M. Snyder wrote, "a physician typically observed his patients without making use of a clinical thermometer or a stethoscope, or without taking the pulse.") The American Medical Association had been founded in Philadelphia as recently as 1847, and among its first works were drafting a Code of Medical Ethics, warning of the dangers of patent medicines and other unproven nostrums, and recommending standards for medical education. But the AMA, made up of physicians whose treatments were based upon the physiology and pathology taught in European medical colleges, was considered too elitist among the vast number of "unorthodox" (an AMA euphemism for "quack") practitioners and the general public. Many years would pass before the organization's influence would be felt.

Mary's classroom work included sessions in pathology, obstetrics and diseases of women and children, pharmacy, anatomy, physiology, principles of surgery, medical law, materia medica, therapeutics, chemistry, and botany. These, "a formidable but necessarily shallow potpourri of studies," wrote Charles Snyder, were conducted by the faculty under the "eclectic" system of medicine. This school was described, more hopefully than realistically, as "borrowing of the best science and techniques" from several other current systems of medicine.

Principal among the systems borrowed from were herbalism and homeopathy, each favoring "noninvasive" treatment of disease such as the use of botanical extracts and small doses of a limited number of chemical substances. Like all the unorthodox approaches to medicine, the eclectics opposed the "dramatic" or "heroic" treatments—bloodletting, blistering, massive use of purgatives such as calomel and similar mercuric compounds—employed by "allopaths," the established medicos of the era.

A favorite example of such "killing measures," as their opponents called them, was that of George Washington, who, as he lay dying in 1799, was attended by the best-educated physicians in the nation. These Harvard and Yale men bled a total of three quarts of his blood, dosed him with subchloride of mercury (calomel), and covered his weakened body with blisters, all such "heroic" treatments to no effect. Such measures, the eclectics and other medical sectarians correctly believed, disregarded the physician's Hippocratic injunction, "First, do not harm."

2

Mary Walker's father, tending sick and injured field workers and neighbors at his Bunker Hill Farm, was probably a herbalist, a follower of the work of New Hampshire farmer and "root doctor" John Thompson (1769–1843). His literal grassroots therapeutics employed the medical properties of native plants for health and longevity, and his teachings had an enormous following for decades after his death. Thompson explained his ideas in his 1848 book, *New Guide to Health, or Botanic Family Physician,* which would have been required reading for Mary as she made use of Alvah's home library.

Besides offering cheap and homegrown treatments, Thompson's every-man-his-own-physician philosophy, which included radical views on the bloodletting medical establishment, would have appealed to Alvah Walker as it did to thousands of others. The New Englander maintained that "regular" physicians were elitists, more interested in money than cures, more interested in excluding "nontraditional" ideas than discovering and embracing the truths within them. He called for the elimination of state licensing for medical practitioners and for the democratization of medicine.

Syracuse Medical College had been founded on a school of medical thought which supposedly borrowed the best theories from the several other "schools" wrestling for eminence in midcentury America. The "eclectic" approach to medicine, an outgrowth of Thompson's herbalism, was founded by a New Yorker named Wooster Beach (1794–1868), an allopathic physician who sought reform in his profession but departed from Thompson's imperious and antagonistic methods. Beach was trained in chemistry, physiology, and pathology and applied these sciences to his botanic-based practice of "reformed medicine." He studied the chemical makeup of plants and developed herbal techniques in treating blood and circulatory problems, fevers, and other ailments. Like all of the medical splinter groups, Beach opposed bleeding and massive doses of mercurics but adapted ideas from regular and folk-loric teachings to arrive at his theories.

By 1845, with the establishment of the Eclectic Medical Institute, Cincinnati became the mecca of Beach's ideas, with eclectic medical schools, usually with small enrollments and faculty, opening in Ohio, the Midwest, and New York State.

At Syracuse Medical College, Mary Walker learned to spurn allopathic measures, a lesson she did not forget in the medical tents of the Civil War when she railed against surgeons adding bloodshed to bloodshed with their often unsystematic and wholesale amputation of wounded limbs. She studied chemistry (with an emphasis on botanic chemical composition), physiology, pathology, hygiene, pharmacy (also with a herbalistic underpinning), and some of the best techniques of the other sectarian medical practices. Among these were hydrotherapy and homeopathy. The former, involving the intensive application of water internally and externally combined with a strenuous regimen of personal hygiene, had given rise to many "water cure" hotels and spas before the Civil War. Homeopathy, a European practice that reached the United States in 1825, had a much larger following. It was based on the idea of intensive study of the patient and his symptoms; a single medicine administered in small, graduated doses was then used to treat the symptoms. Eclectics, like homeopaths, avoided many chemical compounds and favored relatively harmless vegetable substitutes.

In a time of such a divisive array of medical teachings, Mary seemed to have found the eclectic curriculum at Syracuse Medical College satisfying, perhaps because of its liberal

nature, which matched her father's teachings at home, and because the school admitted her, apparently without questioning
her gender. Her eighteen months of study were intensive as
well, much more so than many similarly sectarian colleges,
giving her a substantial—by midcentury standards—medical
education that bolstered her natural self-confidence.

In June 1855, only six years after Elizabeth Blackwell
became America's first female physician, Mary Walker took
her degree—the only female in her graduating class—and at
age twenty-two became one of a handful of women medical
practitioners in the country.

Eclectic

1

In the six months following the triumph of her graduation from Syracuse Medical College, Mary suffered a number of reversals, several of which might have devastated a less resolute twenty-two-year-old woman. For her, failures merely girded her for future battles.

The least of her setbacks she revealed while speaking to an audience about her Civil War experiences in England in 1866. She said that upon finishing her medical training she had hoped to go out to the Crimea, the peninsula in the Black Sea where British and Russian armies were at war. News of the battles at Balaclava and Sebastopol, and the suffering of wounded British troops, had appeared in New York newspapers, and she wanted to volunteer her services, probably inspired by the example of the heroic "Lady with the Lamp," Florence Nightingale. But, she said, by the time she received her degree the war was concluding and the opportunity slipped by.

Instead of this adventuresome idea and probably at her parents' suggestion, she launched her medical career in 1855 in Columbus, Ohio, where a Walker family aunt lived. Columbus had another allure: Only a hundred miles southwest, in Cincinnati, lay the home of the Eclectic Medical Institute, founded in 1845 by the father of eclectic medicine, Wooster Beach. A dean or faculty member at Syracuse may have suggested that she would have a better chance at success as a female physician in the hub and heart of eclecticism than in New York, where all manner of medical sects were in aggressive competition.

Whatever the origin of her Columbus decision, she failed to open a medical practice there and soon returned home. At the invitation of a Syracuse classmate, Albert Miller, she then left Oswego for the town of Rome, sixty miles east, where Miller had opened a medical practice.

2

From the beginning of her career, in both Ohio and New York, Mary Walker encountered not only the existing, standard prejudices of her day, but consciously added to them. In the 1850s American female physicians were viewed as quacks—women who did not know their rightful, biblical place in society and who disrupted the social pattern by insisting on invading a domain that was historically exclusively male. Female physician was a contradiction in terms.

Charles M. Snyder states that the difficulties she met in establishing a medical practice in the face of such sexual intolerance contributed to her assortment of behavioral quirks, but in truth, one of those quirks, the one that identified her all her life, predated her choice of a medical career.

In 1855, at age twenty-three, Mary stood barely five feet tall and weighed perhaps 100 to 120 pounds. Except for a perpetually downturned mouth, she had a pretty, well-scrubbed face devoid of makeup, with wide-set brown eyes and a high forehead framed by shiny auburn hair, sometimes midparted and tucked behind her ears, later arranged in a swept-back bob. At this time in her life she had not abandoned all feminine touches: She occasionally wore a lacy bodice and white silk neckerchief, wore flowers in her hair and sometimes a small hat—one resembling a bowler with an ostrich feather decoration.

But these slight nods toward femininity aside, by the time she moved to Rome, New York, in the fall of 1855, her choice of dress was increasingly masculine. This marked the beginning of a fifty-year dress evolution to a time when she would wear a swallowtail coat over trousers, a boiled white shirt and stiff collar, necktie, waistcoat (with a watch chain across the front), and a silk topper.

Her lifelong "reform dress" battle began with Alvah Walker's ideas that this daughters would work the Bunker Hill Farm alongside him and their brother and not be impeded by heavy petticoats, skirts, whalebone corsets ("the vital organs of women are so compressed by stays or corsets that health is impaired and life shortened," she would say), and the other accouterments of female garb. Mary, apparently alone among her sisters, took the idea to heart. She knew the ideas advanced by Amelia Jenks Bloomer, one of the participants in the Seneca Falls Women's Rights Convention of 1848. Bloomer, in her popular temperance newspaper *Lily*, railed against cumbersome female clothing and advocated a daring ensemble of loose bodices, Turkish-style pantaloons gathered at the ankle, and a dress cut to above the knee, and Walker elaborated on these ideas. She was not satisfied with pantaloons, perhaps viewing them, as many did, as too suggestive of a harem, and designed her own straight, tailored, trousers supported by galluses over which she favored a long-sleeved, high-necked, loose-waisted tuniclike dress, its skirt falling just below the trouser knees, and stockings without elastics or bands underneath.

This outfit, while not thoroughly masculinizing her appearance (that came later), signaled to others that she was "eccentric," no matter the soundness of her arguments that the weight, length, and strictures of typical female dress were not only uncomfortable but unsanitary and unhealthy. She said women's garments "shackled and enfeebled" their wearers and threatened their very sanity, that "a woman in the ordinary Dress expends more vitality in wearing such Dress, than a horse does wearing his harness." She carried her argument to such heights as to alienate the suffrage activists when she said, "The greatest sorrows from which women suffer today are those physical, moral and mental ones that are cause by their unhygienic manner of dressing! The want of the ballot is but a toy by comparison."

Over the years, in lecture halls, magazine articles, and in her mysteriously titled 1871 book *Hit*, she refined her ideas by employing medical or pseudomedical jargon, finding even more evils in traditional dress and fashion.

"The snug fit of the waist of the Dress or corsets," she wrote, "prevents freedom of motion, of respiration, digestion, assimilative circulation of the blood. And of the nervo-vital fluid. It prevents the freedom of the muscles of the lower part of the chest, and the upper part of the legs; producing a weariness of the bony structure, both at their origin and insertion."

Of hoops in skirts she said "there is the atmospheric pressure to overcome . . . when walking against the wind, and the same to resist when walking from the same."

According to Mary, the weight of petticoats and skirts was unhealthy; women's shoes caused corns; elastics in stockings and wristbands impeded circulation; long skirts were unhygienic because they dragged on the ground, collecting dirt and nameless substances from the street; and the uneven distribution of women's clothing gave rise to neuralgia, chilblains, and rheumatism.

Nor did hairstyles escape her critical eye: "There is no way the hair can be worn without injury," she said, "save in a perfectly free and flowing manner. . . . free from chignon, extra braids, frizzes, curls, rats, mice, combs, pins, etc. etc."

She determined that conventional female dress impeded a happy marriage, affecting both wife and husband. To begin with, she said, "Scarcely a woman can be found old enough to marry who is not afflicted with some ailment produced by wearing an unhygienic Dress. From the crown of the head to the soles of the feet, the women are unhealthfully attired." These "thousand perplexities of fashionable Dress wear so upon the temper of a woman, that she cannot be amiable." Of her mate: ". . . many men will not marry, because of the voluminous and numerous Dresses, with their other paraphernalia, requires a small fortune to replenish the ever changing fashionable styles."

However, she warned those men who wished to keep women captive, laced into their whalebone corsets: "A husband has no more right to dictate about the cut of his wife's clothes, than has the wife to interfere with the husband's, and it is time that the barbarous ideas of men assuming such prerogatives, were swept away, and the inherent *right* of woman to dress as she pleases established."

As for herself, when chastised her for her "reform dress," she liked to say, "I don't wear men's clothes, I wear my own clothes."

What God Hath Joined

1

Albert Miller, M.D., a man who indisputably influenced Mary Walker's attitudes toward marriage and divorce, is a shadowy figure. He left little in the way of a record—his age, birthplace, family, travels, even his physical appearance, are unknown. She met him as a classmate at Syracuse Medical College, where he had a reputation as a charismatic orator and a freethinker in the Alvah Walker mode—no doubt the source of her attraction to him.

The two may have courted during their Syracuse time together and must have kept in touch by letter after their graduation, when Miller set up a practice in Rome and she was testing the medical opportunities in Ohio. In any event, their reunion in Rome, at some point in the fall of 1855, was apparently warm since they married within a month or two of her arrival there.

The ceremony took place in the Walker home in Oswego, and while the family was nominally Methodist, a Unitarian minister officiated, probably because of certain departures from the Christian ceremony that she insisted upon. She appeared at her wedding dressed in trousers and frock coat and insisted that any reference to the bride's obligation to obey her spouse be removed from the service. "How barbarous the very idea of one equal promising to be the slave of another, instead of both entering life's greatest drama as intelligent equal parties," she would later write, very much in the manner and spirit of the Seneca Falls Declaration. She also felt that the "What God has joined together" part of the ceremony hypocritical: "He has nothing to do with the matter," she said, "any more than suffering their consummation and continuance." Any assumption that a woman needed a man's protection, she made clear, was "a male myth and subterfuge for male tyranny," and "any law or custom that deprives a being of individuality, in any of the relations of life, contravenes the great laws of Deity, thus bringing evil results."

She made one tiny concession to the institutionalized norms of marriage by occasionally using Miller's name, but only as Dr. Mary Miller-Walker, never as Dr. or Mrs. Mary Miller. She later wrote, "A woman's name is as dear to her as a man's is to him, and custom ought, and will prevail, where each will keep their own names when they marry, and allow the children at a certain age to decide which name they will prefer." She even offered a tongue-in-cheek suggestion: "A woman must be called *Mrs.* to let all the world know she is married, and if there is a necessity for this, why not call a man *Misterer* for the purpose of enlightening the world as to his condition?"

The newlyweds rented rooms on Dominick Street in Rome and set up house and offices there. Biographer Charles Snyder states that, "At the outset Mary appears to have been an affectionate wife, anxious to please and assist her husband" in both their domestic and professional lives. But, while Miller does not seem to have objected to Mary's quirks—her wedding outfit or her use, or not, of his name—the marriage was doomed from the start. Albert's thinking was freer than hers on at least one major issue: fidelity. His reputation as a libertine may have preceded their wedding but she learned about it afterward, and when she found out that he was an adulterer (we do not know exactly when in their six-year marriage she learned of it) she ordered him to vacate the house. By March 1861 they had separated, and in September a preliminary divorce decree, on grounds of adultery, was granted to Mary by the state of New York. After that, somehow the case sputtered, for reasons unknown but probably because of disputes between the two, and the divorce would not become final for another five years.

2

Queen Victoria, Mary Walker's personal icon representing virtue, love, marriage, and fidelity (in that order) rose to England's throne in 1837. Her marriage in 1840 to Prince Albert, duke of Saxe-Coburg-Gotha, produced nine children, and in her sixty-three-year reign (forty of them as a widow), she became a paragon of private and public honor and of honesty and devotion to duty and family. These were all Mary's adopted ideals and when she wrote of them she did so as a true child of the Victorian age and a disciple of the woman who gave it its name.

Her devotion to Victorian ideals and her unhappy venture into matrimony produced an assemblage of philosophical observations and beliefs, many of them found in her 1871 book, *Hit: Essays on Women's Rights*. She researched marriage customs and cited examples from Turkey, Scotland, Russia, Assyria, Persia, Armenia, Norway, the Malabar Coast, Jamaica, Egypt, Siberia, Japan, India, Arabia, as well as the North American Indians, the inhabitants of New South Wales, and several of the American states. But the main tenets of her ideas on marriage were haunted by the ghosts of the faithful queen of England and of the deceitful Albert Miller.

"True conjugal companionship is the greatest blessing of which mortals can conceive in this life," she wrote, but warned that while love was essential to such a companionship, "there cannot be love without respect, and there cannot be respect unless there is implicit confidence."

Love and lust were too often confused, she said, perhaps giving a clue to Albert Miller's sexual expectations and her reaction to them in their marriage. Too many people, she said, "have so little of Love, and so much of excitability of sexuality, that great wrongs are inflicted on soul and body, to an incalculable extent"; and, "The grossest people, those not far removed from the animals, cannot understand that there can be, that it is possible in human nature, for a soul love, unmixed with sensuality."

Miller's faithlessness is clearly the source of Mary's observation that "thousands of women have been accused of being jealous, when they are not so at all, for they were sorrowing over a husband's infidelity." Such women, she said, "could not *prove* his [the husband's] vileness, according to the codes of *man,* but it was proved to them, in the severing of the invisible magnetic cable which can *never* again be so united as to possess its former strength and power."

As to the matter of divorce, she wrote in *Hit:* "To be deprived of a Divorce is like being shut up in a prison because some one attempted to kill you. . . . It is just as honorable to get out of matrimonial trouble *legally,* as to be freed from any other wrong. If is it right to be legally married, it is right to be legally Divorced."

Ultimately, she reversed her stand, taken at the time of her marriage to Miller, that a certain biblical admonition in the ceremonial vows was "hypocritical." In 1871, she wrote, "'What God hath joined together, let not man put asunder.' The Bible has no command that is more sacred than this, not even the one *'thou shalt not kill.'*"

Orator

1

Now alone and with rent to pay, Mary eked out a living as a horse-and-buggy doctor, pulling teeth at a quarter each, delivering babies (one of the few medical procedures entrusted to women, usually a midwife), consulting with women on problems that would be embarrassing to confide to a male medico, lancing boils, and patching up minor cuts and scrapes.

On March 8, 1860, she bought a classified ad in the *Rome Sentinel*, headed **FEMALE PHYSICIAN:**

DR. MARY WALKER HAS REMOVED TO NO. 48
DOMINICK STREET OPPOSITE THE "ARCADE," OVER
MESSRS. H. S. AND W. O. SHELLEY'S CLOTHING STORE.

She expressed her gratitude "to the Romans for their liberal patronage," and gave her hours: 7–8 A.M., 1–3, and 6–8 P.M.

Within her notice, the *Sentinel* apologized for seeming to

give a "puff" for one physician over another, but said, "Those, however, who prefer the skill of a female physician to that of the male, have now an excellent opportunity to make their choice."

Late in 1856, not long after her ill-fated venture into marriage, Mary found a like-minded friend and an outlet for her dress-reform ideas. While attending to her meager medical practice in Rome, she began subscribing to *Sibyl: A Review of the Tastes, Errors, and Fashions of Society,* a new fortnightly magazine for women published in Middletown, New York.

The founder and editor of *Sibyl,* Lydia Sayer Hasbrouck, was a dynamic thirty-year-old New Yorker, a hydropathic physician, temperance lecturer, and women's dress reformer. In about 1849, among her many innovations, she invented a daring female costume featuring a knee-length skirt over pantaloons, an outfit that seems to have predated the similar design made prominent by Amelia Jenks Bloomer. (Were it not for Bloomer's louder advocacy of her "Turkish style," so it was said, the female pantaloons might have been called "hasbroucks.")

Just a few months before Mary began writing for *Sibyl,* Hasbrouck's marriage was written up in the Elmira, New York, *Advertiser,* with details eerily similar to those of Mary Walker and Albert Miller's ceremony. "John W. Hasbrouck Esq., of the Whig Press, has married a Doctor, which sounds rather strange," the newspaper reported, "but the age is a progressive one and he will be to no expense for a 'family physician.'" The wedding took place in Warwick on July 27, 1856, with the bride "dressed in the 'reform costume'—skirt of white India [fabric], with pants of white satin; a basque of brocade silk (color of ashes of roses) trimmed with dress lace; no ornaments except a simple breast-pin." The ceremony "was performed by themselves," the report continued: "The bride ignored that part of the accustomed marriage which demands of woman undue subjection and obedience, yet promising equally with the groom to stand true to his side in all the duties of life—each appealing to the other for their approval and each consenting to the terms adopted by themselves."

Mary's debut as a writer for *Sibyl* appeared on January 1, 1857, with a letter hailing a dress-reform convention to be held at Canastota, a village a few miles east of Syracuse. She later became something of a correspondent for the magazine, attending and writing on the Dress Reform Association meeting in Syracuse and in the spring of 1860, the DRA meeting in Waterloo, New York, during which she was elected one of the nine vice presidents of the organization.

2

While railing against fashionable and "accepted" dress customs continued as her great crusade, her repertoire of issues grew from her association with Hasbrouck and enabled her to launch a new pursuit in 1858. Lecturing, whether before a handful of curious, semishocked ladies at a social tea or onstage facing a mixed crowd in a rented hall, gave her an outlet that would occupy her far more than the practice of medicine. What began as an incidental sideline became her chief source of income in years to come.

No details of their friendship have survived, but Mary Walker and Lydia Hasbrouck were almost alone among the women's rights sisterhood to continue to wear the reform-dress outfit throughout their lives. Each was a temperance fighter, each devoted her career to secular medicine, and each was inspired by the women's rights ideas advanced at the Seneca Falls Convention of 1848.

3

Mary began her oratorical career with a speech on her pet issue, dress reform, at home before a gathering of "hugely crinolined Oswegians" but soon grew comfortable in speaking on a variety of issues that taught her audiences what she meant by her proclamation, "It is my motto to live by my principles."

The range of her oratory, amplified over the forty years that followed her Oswego lecture, ran the gamut—or gauntlet—of the most contentious issues of her era. She spoke on the evils of alcohol and tobacco, on love, marriage, divorce, labor laws, religion, immorality, politics, "morally unfortunate women," venereal disease, war, diet, abortion, and inhumane prison conditions. She spoke on such lesser matters as a "safe and sane" Independence Day celebration and the terrible maimings caused by fireworks. She also railed against vaccinations for smallpox, claims for which she said were exaggerated and done for money, and late in her life pronounced as humbug claims that germs caused tuberculosis.

She often compounded the contentious nature of her subjects with her personalized approach to them. On the issue of women's suffrage, among the most heated concerns of the women's rights movement, she said, "No country is free where women cannot vote," but minimized this proclamation by comparing the vote to the "physical, moral and mental" disease caused by women's "unhygienic manner of dressing."

(Privately she referred to the suffragists as "sainted morons," and said their campaign detracted from more important women's issues—the precise charge made by the suffragists against Mary's dress-reform fixation.)

For all the diffuse and variegated subjects that concerned her and gave her unlimited resources for her lectures and occasional *Sybil* writings, Mary was focused on the need for social and political equality between the sexes. She was never more at home than when urging her largely female audiences to "throw aside their embroidery and read Mental Philosophy, Moral Science and Physiology," urging women to "go to a smith and have their dressical and dietetical chains severed so they more go forth free, sensible women."

Her own experiences as a farm girl in Oswego convinced her that "Not only every son but every daughter should be given a practical knowledge of some business whereby they can support themselves," and she advanced the radical idea that women should receive equal pay for equal work instead of "the pittance paid for woman's work." She said that while males "retired" from their businesses, it was an exclusive male privilege, that woman's work was never done yet received neither recompense nor respect:

One, and I may say the great reason why the mass of women are so dissatisfied with their domestic duties is because they are painfully conscious of the inability of men to duly appreciate the thousand cares, thoughts, and anxieties of their position. Too well do women know the great mass of men feel that if they earn the money, they have performed the nine-tenths part of living, and whatever a woman does is only of minor consideration.

In the spring of 1859 a national scandal occurred that neatly illustrated several of Mary Walker's convictions on marriage, adultery, and prevailing attitudes separating the sexes. On February 27 of that year, New York Congressman Daniel Sickles, a powerful Tammany politician and friend of President James Buchanan, shot and killed United States District Attorney Philip Barton Key, grandson of the author of the national anthem, "The Star-Spangled Banner."

The killing took place in Lafayette Square, a short walk from the White House, and was the culmination of an affair Key was having with Sickles's wife. The congressman, after receiving an anonymous note telling him that Key and Teresa Sickles were having "clandestine meetings" in a rented house, forced his wife to confess to the affair. A few days later Sickles armed himself with two derringers and a five-shot revolver, saw Key walking down the street, rushed out and shot the attorney in the groin and chest as Key begged for mercy.

The nation's newspapers were filled with the "Washington Tragedy"—*Leslie's Illustrated* sold more than two hundred thousand copies of its issue devoted to the incident and *The New York Times* ran daily updates on "The Sickles Tragedy" across six columns of its front page. Virtually all the coverage sided with the cuckolded congressman—the *Albany Evening Statesman* was almost alone in New York in hinting that Sickles himself "had a reputation for anything *but* integrity, honor, morality and manhood." The paper hinted that his own adulterous affairs made him a hypocritical example of a vengeful husband.

The trial of Daniel Sickles for the murder of Philip Barton Key opened on April 4, 1859 (with no women allowed in the courtroom since the testimony was considered too potentially salacious for delicate ears), before an all-male jury. Sickles's eight lawyers—among them Edwin M. Stanton, soon to be Lincoln's secretary of war—employed the then uncommon insanity defense in convincing the jury that their client had been driven crazy by learning of his wife's dalliance with Key. On April 27 the verdict of "not guilty" was announced to nearly everyone's expectation and satisfaction.*

Mary Walker, a lonely voice in the Upstate New York wilderness, had her own marriage ruined by infidelity, which she used as footing to write about the notorious case. In a *Sybil* article she objected to the biased press coverage over Teresa Sickles's "debauchery" and "iniquitous behavior" while making no reference to her husband's reputation as a woman-izer. Contrary to public opinion on the case, she saw Teresa as the one to be pitied. "Never," she wrote, "until women are better educated physiologically, until they are considered something besides a drudge or a doll—until they have all the social, edu-cational and political advantages that men enjoy—in a word, equality with men—shall we consider vice in our sex more culpable than in man."

Daniel Sickles commanded a brigade of New York volun-teers at the opening of the Civil War, served at Chancel-lorsville and other battles, and became commanding general of the Third Corps of the Union army at Gettysburg. During

---

* Sickles and Teresa reconciled after the trial but she died a social out-cast in 1867 at age thirty-one.

this fighting a twelve-pound Confederate artillery shell took off most of his right leg. The mangled limb was amputated and Sickles presented it in a coffinlike box to the army's Medical Museum in Washington, D.C., with a note, "With the compliments of Major General D.E.S." He visited his leg periodically until the end of his life in 1914.

He was awarded the Medal of Honor in 1897 for displaying "most conspicuous gallantry on the field vigorously contesting the advance of the enemy and continuing to encourage his troops after being himself severely wounded."

Mary Walker, who had a few things to say about Sickles, would later have a few other things to say about battlefield amputations and Medals of Honor.

The Lines Are Drawn

1

In the spring of 1860 Mary sought to make final her divorce from Albert Miller and traveled to Iowa where a former Oswegian and lawyer friend of the Walker family resided. She remained in the state nearly a year, but despite her efforts and that of her lawyer friend, failed to find a court that would grant the divorce.

While details of the escapade are scarce, she apparently did succeed in another battle arena, managing to alienate the staff of a collegiate institute near the northeastern Iowa town of Delhi where she attempted to enroll in an all-male rhetoric class. With a handful of fellow freethinkers she is said to have led a march in protest through the town streets.

The Miller matter continued to haunt her. As late as 1885 Albert Miller was inquiring after Mary's welfare but she persisted in calling him a "villain" and "the vile Miller" and would have nothing to do with him. Her experience with him had soured her forever on marriage—and men—and ever after, in her public lectures she spoke angrily on the unfaithful husband. At one point she even declared that a husband who had relations with other women transferred his unchastity to his children and that many deformities in infants were caused by such sexual excesses and abuses.

2

While struggling to earn a living in Rome, and during her frequent visits with her family in Oswego, Mary assiduously followed the news of the looming national crisis. Her parents, always staunch abolitionists, taught their children about the evils of slavery, and *Uncle Tom's Cabin,* Harriet Beecher Stowe's 1857 runaway bestseller was no doubt among Alvah Walker's assortment of books, together with the teachings of the antislavery crusader William Lloyd Garrison.

In 1859, slavery, which Thomas Jefferson (a slave owner) had said might be "the knell of the Union," was a tolling issue. Its reverberations were heard everywhere in populous New York, where the antislavery movement originated in the 1830s; in New England, home of many of the most eloquent abolitionists, notably Garrison and Frederick Douglass; and in the South, where the "peculiar institution" (as Thoreau called it) was the cornerstone of the cotton-plantation economy and the social system that grew up around it. In the South, slavery gave rise to persistent talk of state rights, of popular sovereignty, and of secession from the Union.

The issue was poisonous, the source of a corrosive antagonism between individuals, factions, political parties, and the states of the North and South. It was resistant to compromise, and it was explosive: "Slavery will not be overthrown without excitement, a most tremendous excitement," Garrison wrote in his newspaper, *The Liberator*.

Six months after the Dan Sickles trial and Mary Walker's condemnation of the biased newspaper journalism on the case, a prelude to Garrison's "tremendous excitement" occurred in Virginia at the confluence of the Potomac and Shenandoah Rivers. There, at dawn on October 16, 1859, John Brown, a fifty-nine-year-old Bible thumper with a spade beard and a touch of insanity in his steely eyes, led a gang of twenty-one men, six of them black, in a doomed raid of the United States arsenal at Harper's Ferry. After 36 hours of fighting and 17 deaths (10 of them Brown's raiders, including 2 of his sons) the siege ended. Brown and five of his men were taken prisoner, while the others escaped.

John Brown's trial for treason, murder, and conspiring with slaves, ended on November 2 with "God's Angry Man" sentenced to death. He was taken by wagon, sitting on his coffin, to the Charles Town, Virginia (later West Virginia) scaffold and was hanged at ll:30 A.M. on December 2, 1859.

"You may dispose of me very easily; I am nearly disposed of now," he testified a few days before his execution, "but this question is still to be settled—this negro question I mean—the end of that is not yet." Then, as a sort of last testament, he said, "I, John Brown am now quite certain that the crimes of this guilty land will never be purged away but with Blood."

3

No stretch of the imagination is required to imagine the Walker clan in Oswego gathered around the dinner table while father Alvah, the veteran Underground Railroader, declaimed on John Brown's unfortunately violent but righteous attempt to galvanize the black populace to revolt against its oppressors. He would call Brown, his slain sons, and companions, martyrs and admire their courage in bringing the slavery question to an echoing shout for freedom, and all his family would have agreed.

The Walkers (including Mary, then in Iowa seeking to put a legal end to her marriage) were also riveted by the news that followed John Brown's mad raid, of the critical opening, on April 23, 1860, of the Democratic National Convention in Charleston, South Carolina. Newspaper reports out of sultry Charleston characterized the city as the stronghold of secessionist sentiment, of the bitter feuds within the party, of the "fire-eaters" and their hatred of the leading Democratic candidate for the presidency, Illinois Senator Stephen A. Douglas. His nomination, his adherents said, was vital if the Union was to be preserved, but southern extremists wanted nothing of the "Little Giant," despite his record of friendship with the South and his support of popular sovereignty—leaving the slavery issue to be resolved by the states. He had debated the fundamental issue of slavery with Illinois Republican Congressman Abraham Lincoln in 1859 and disagreed with Lincoln's biblical quotation on the growing sectional conflict that "a house divided against itself cannot stand." This, he said, was proof that Lincoln was an abolitionist, a radical with dangerous ideas of racial equality. But to the real radicals, the southern fire-eaters, Douglas was a "Unionist," a word anathema to those who wanted a do-or-die proslavery candidate.

In the end the southern delegates walked out after the convention's platform committee refused to admit a plank calling for federal protection of slavery in the territories. The convention deadlocked and moved to Baltimore in June where the delegates split again, one faction nominating Douglas, the other James Buchanan's vice president, John C. Breckinridge.

In May 1860, between the Democrats' Charleston and Baltimore conventions, the Republicans convened in Chicago and nominated Abraham Lincoln on the third ballot. The party's platform upheld southern slavery, called for an end to slavery in the territories awaiting statehood, and denounced as treason all schemes for "disunion."

But to southern radicals, Lincoln's nomination and the party's platform were considered an overt act justifying secession. A month after Lincoln's election in November, South Carolina issued an Ordinance of Secession, followed in a few weeks by Mississippi, Florida, Alabama, Georgia, Louisiana, and Texas. Between April and June 1861, four other states— Virginia, Arkansas, North Carolina, and Tennessee—joined the Confederacy.

Any opportunity for peace disappeared in cannon smoke at Fort Sumter, in the harbor of Charleston, South Carolina, on April 12, 1861, when southern batteries open fired on the fort's federal garrison and forced its surrender thirty-four hours later.

A month later, the Confederate capital was moved from Montgomery, Alabama, to Richmond, Virginia, the richest and most populous southern state and the theater for most of the opening battles. Richmond lay a hundred miles from Washington, and "On to Richmond!" became the first federal battle cry.

The lines were drawn, the stage set for a bloodletting no-body envisioned: three million men served in the two armies during 2,200 separate engagements—skirmishes to full-fledged battles fought from Vermont to New Mexico Territory—with 430 soldiers dying every day on average until the war ran its course after four years.

Washington, 1861

1

For twenty-nine-year-old Mary, the beginning of hostilities offered several opportunities, principally a chance to work, if she could find a physician's post somewhere. She could leave Rome, an unproductive medical practice, and a broken marriage, and honor her conviction and that of her family, that preservation of the Union was a vital cause. Duty weighed heavily on her. She later wrote, "My reason for my acts has been a strong conviction of that which I believed was right. I was naturally timid as a girl, but had to overcome this through strong convictions of duty and I have felt that I must do what I believed was right regardless of consequences. I do not deserve credit for standing up to my principles for I could not do otherwise."

While she left no details on her plan to go to Washington and seek a medical commission, she talked of the idea with her family and father Alvah, especially, supported her. He urged her to resume the journal she had given up on as a child, as if foreseeing that Mary's experiences in the war would somehow be significant.

His daughter's experiences were significant beyond Alvah's dreams but the journal would not be written. Mary, at some undetermined point after the war did make some preliminary notes toward an autobiography, and committed to paper an undated, disorganized document she titled "Incidents Connected with the Army,"* which provided some insights and anecdotes of her service but little detail of her motivations or day-to-day experiences.

In "Incidents" she wrote:

> While I was in the army my father wrote me urging that I keep a daily journal which I attempted to do for a time but there was so much to be written and I was so weary that I abandoned it after a brief time much to my regret since there are many times that it is very difficult to fix and names that it is impossible to remember. . . . Those who had no experience in the time of our terrible war can not possibly understand the weariness and consequent want of energy to make exertions not absolutely imperative at the time.

The circumstance that drove Mary to pack her Rome belongings and head to Washington for the decisive turning point of her life was the event that unfolded twenty-six miles

---

* The original of which, twenty-eight legal-sized typed pages, is in the Walker Papers at Syracuse University's E. S. Bird Library Special Collections Research Center.

southwest of the capital in July 1861. This was the point of no return that drove home the fact that a real killing war had begun.

2

Both the north and south, convinced of their superiority and certain of victory, were eager to fight. The newly organized Confederacy was anxious to transfer its capital from Montgomery, Alabama, to Richmond, Virginia, a move northern politicians viewed as treasonous and thought must be stopped. To do so, the first attempt to capture Richmond began on July 16, when Union General Irvin McDowell moved south across the Potomac with thirty-five thousand troops, including gaudy, Algerian-style Zouaves in red pantaloons and kilted New York Highlanders, most of them young three-month volunteers in a motley of brown, gray, and blue homemade uniforms. Their service had begun after the fall of Fort Sumter the previous April, when President Lincoln issued a call for seventy-five thousand volunteers to end the "rebellion," and all were anxious to go home.

McDowell's mission was to seize the railroad junction at Manassas, defended by Confederate General Pierre G. T. Beauregard, McDowell's West Point classmate and friend, with twenty thousand equally untested troops commanded by General Joseph E. Johnston and massed behind a creek called Bull Run. On a muggy July 21, the Federals attacked Beauregard's left flank and won an early advantage until rebel reinforcements under General Johnston arrived from Harper's Ferry and forced McDowell's retreat toward Washington. Joining the exodus and turning it into chaos were throngs of Washingtonians who had ventured out on horseback, in carriages and wagons, with picnic baskets, bottles of wine, and spyglasses, to watch the battle from east of Bull Run Creek as if it were a fireworks exhibition. When the fight turned against the Federals, the civilians fled in panic, clotting the roads and slowing the ambulance wagons and troops wandering back to the capital. There, Pennsylvania Avenue was packed with frightened citizens elaborating on the rumors of a rout—"the population of a doomed city, listening for the thundering guns, the pounding cavalry, the shouts of the victorious rebel army," as Margaret Leech wrote in her *Reveille in Washington.*

Fortunately, the rebels chose not to pursue the stragglers and instead picked through the loot, a huge amount of ammunition and small arms, on the battlefield.

The Union lost close to three thousand men killed, wounded, and missing at the First Battle of Bull Run; the Confederates about two thousand.

3

By the time Mary Walker reached Washington in October 1861, three months after Bull Run, the country was girded for full-fledged war and the capital had transformed into one of the most heavily fortified cities on the continent, eventually to be surrounded in a thirty-seven-mile circle by nearly a hundred cannon emplacements and sixty forts. This epicenter of war was also among the shabbiest and crime-ridden seats of government in the civilized world. Sixty years after its founding, Washington consisted of six federal buildings (the Capitol, its dome unfinished and bedecked with scaffolding; the Post Office, Patent Office, Treasury, Smithsonian Institution, and Executive Mansion) plus shacks, sheds, and warehouses; a few respectable hotels—notably Willard's on Fourteenth Street*—plus restaurants, saloons, and a number of churches, schools, and shops along Pennsylvania Avenue. That great thoroughfare was cobbled but most of the town's roads and streets were unpaved mud bogs giving off a nearly palpable stench, from horse manure, a failing sewage system, the habit of emptying "slops" in the gutters, throwing dead animals into a canal connected to the Potomac, and hauling carts of raw night soil to a dump less than a mile north of the White House. All these conspired to provide the town and its forty thousand citizens (150,000 by war's end) the ideal matrix for the breeding of cholera, typhoid, dysentery, and other diseases in addition to malaria, which was already commonplace in the swampy city.

Now, in the aftermath of Bull Run, Washington was burdened with battle casualties, with hospital wards and surgeries opening in public buildings, churches, private homes, the Patent Office, in tents on vacant lots. Physicians were in desperately short supply, a circumstance Mary Walker knew well when she visited the Department of the Army, on the west side of the Executive Mansion, in October 1861, and was ushered into the office of Lieutenant Colonel Edward Davis Townsend, the assistant adjutant general.

A patient, competent officer, Colonel Townsend, a West Point graduate of the Class of 1837, later represented the army at the various funerals for President Lincoln. He left no record of his first meeting with Mary, nor did she with him,

---

* Where, in late 1861, Mrs. Julia Ward Howe stayed and wrote the verses to "The Battle Hymn of the Republic."

but she spoke with him and presented her documents and credentials, volunteering her services as an assistant surgeon "to a regiment in the field."

Townsend, a stiff-backed professional soldier with a receding hairline, startling blue eyes, and a wide slash of mouth, stared, puzzled and probably vaguely amused, but concealed both emotions as he read her papers and absorbed her words and appearance. Here was a pretty, tiny, well-scrubbed, intensely businesslike woman, age twenty-nine, her short black hair severely parted in the middle and gathered behind her ears, dressed in a heavy black overcoat buttoned over a white, high-necked shirtwaist, waistcoat, gray trousers, and a dark skirt that fell below the knees.

Mary would later describe herself at this time, writing as if someone else was observing and reporting on her, as having a fine complexion, "sparkling eyes and a profusion of dark curls." She said she was "very small, only a little over five feet tall, well rounded as a girl but never plump. . . ." A sympathetic New York newspaper accentuated this, stating that in the opening period of her war service she was "dressed in male habiliments, with the exception of a girlish-looking straw hat, decked off with an ostrich feather, with a petite figure and feminine features . . . she carries herself amid the camp with the jaunty air of dignity well-calculated to receive the sincere respect of the soldiers."

Since, early on, she became a conspicuous figure in Washington for her credentials as a bona fide female doctor of medicine, and for her mode of dress, the press of that city took repeated notice of her, writing mostly affirmative notices on her "positive attitude," her generosity, drive, tirelessness, and sense of humor.

But these attributes, some of them observed by Colonel Townsend of the Adjutant General's Office, did not help; he was not authorized to handle her request and referred her to the War Department. There she received a frosty reception, some perfunctory words about her "lack of surgical experience," and a denial of her request for a commission.

These first steps into the bureaucratic maze of Washington in 1861 were at least educational for Mary, even though the learning process was disheartening. Her civilian medical career had foundered from day one, for a simple, unmysterious reason: She was a woman trying to find a place in a virtually all-male professional arena. But in wartime, with the well-advertised critical need for physicians in volunteer regiments and in behind-the-lines camp hospitals, she imagined her gender would be of no consequence. She thought her dress habits would be viewed as practical for the work to be done, and her education more than adequate.

Unfortunately, none of these reasonable notions were shared by the medical hierarchy in wartime Washington.

Although unknown to Mary at the time, there was irony in her brief visit with the assistant adjutant general. Shortly before her visit, Colonel Townsend had made a recommendation to Winfield Scott, the general-in-chief of the army. Townsend suggested that the army ought to award a special medal to those displaying particular heroism in the war. General Scott rejected the idea—it smacked of British custom—but the idea did not die.

Mary would meet both Colonel Townsend and his medal idea in time to come.

MEDICINE AND THE UNION ARMY

Mary Walker's eclectic medical training, her minimal surgical experience, her inability to take "no" for an answer, and, above all these, her gender and personal dress code, threw her against many Union army protocols and ingrained customs, particularly those of the army's medical branch.

In 1861, at the outset of the Civil War, the army numbered seventeen thousand men, most of them scattered in camps and forts on the western frontier. The army's medical department consisted of a surgeon general, a standing cadre of medical officers numbering thirty surgeons and eighty-four assistant surgeons, unattached to any regimental command and rotated wherever they were needed. No hospital corps existed; nursing and hospital duties were performed by soldiers temporarily detailed to such duty.

As the war progressed, the Union's medical services expanded but never kept pace with the growth of the army's volunteer enlistments, particularly in the number of experienced surgeons needed in the battle zones.

In her wartime service Mary Walker encountered
a bewildering medical ladder of command: the
Regular Army Medical Corps; an echelon of volunteer surgeons and assistant surgeons; another of
regimental surgeons and assistant surgeons commissioned by state governors rather than Congress or the president; and a level of physicians
known as "contract" surgeons. These held no commission but received pay as first lieutenants and
worked in the general hospitals in the North, often
while continuing their private practices.

"Competent or incompetent, surgically skilled or not,
vast numbers of doctors were needed to treat the
army of injured," wrote John Wesley Wells in his
study of the medical services of the Civil War
forces. "So great was the demand that more than
12,500 physicians from the North and 3,000 from
the South, not including unknown numbers of
volunteers, were called into service in either field
or civilian hospitals."

Wells states that most of the men who served as regimental surgeons and assistant surgeons were
commissioned by state governors and were "usually only capable of general medical practice.

Being surgically inept, they frequently botched the simplest of surgical operations and often caused wounded soldiers more harm than good."

Of the "contract surgeon," the title Mary Walker sought so relentlessly, the author states that more than five thousand five hundred civilian doctors assisted the medical department during the war, many routinely staffing general hospitals, others providing emergency assistance. Among contract surgeons, Wells writes, "were some of the nation's most prominent doctors" but in a time of "overwhelming numbers of casualties," he wrote, an inordinate number of "quacks, cultists, and practitioners of questionable ethics" volunteered for service.

Mary Walker's single greatest wartime obstacle was precisely this—being labeled a quack and cultist for her nontraditional training; this added to the overwhelming burden of being a female in male dress.

Indiana Hospital

1

Late in 1861, a month or so after the War Department rejected her appeal for service in the field, Mary Walker volunteered as a civilian medical worker in Washington's temporary "Indiana Hospital." The facility, so called since it was occupied primarily by Indiana troops, had been set up in a wing of the United States Patent Office.

She wrote to her family in Oswego claiming to be an "Assistant Physician & Surgeon" among about eighty patients, "five very nice lady nurses and a number of gentlemen nurses." She said, "Every soul in the Hospital has to abide by my orders as much as though Dr. Green gave them . . ."

Most of this, to say the least, was wishful thinking.

She had walked into the Indiana Hospital ward and found the surgeon-in-charge, Dr. J. N. Green, working alone among his wounded and sick patients, his predecessor having recently died, he said, "from overwork." Green does not seem to have taken more than cursory notice of Mary's gender or dress. He examined her medical school credentials, was persuaded that they were better than many others he had read, and was impressed by her sense of duty and determination to serve. He welcomed her but could offer her nothing more than work as an unpaid, uncommissioned volunteer.

Walker biographer Charles M. Snyder states that her tasks at the Indiana Hospital and elsewhere during the war were primarily those of therapist, counselor, amanuensis—letter writer—and "confessor" to battle fatigued, homesick soldiers, men facing futures as amputees, some near death. Mary insisted she did more than such nurselike duties. She made rounds, she said, prescribed treatments and medications, assisted in surgeries and in diagnosing ailments such as smallpox for purposes of quarantine, and in general served as a regular assistant surgeon.

Her superior, J. N. Green, first of a number of medical men who praised her work, seemed to support her contention when he wrote to the army's surgeon general in support of Mary's appeal for appointment as assistant surgeon. "I need and desire her assistance here very much believing as I do that she is well qualified for the position." He referred to her "valuable assistance" and portrayed her as "an intelligent and judicious Physician."

While the shortage of medical personnel often made it necessary to change dressings, bathe patients, and swamp floors, Mary avoided such menial work when nurses and orderlies were available. She was a *physician,* she insisted, and disassociated herself from mere nursing—a new, makeshift, line of work requiring no particular skills or education.

Such insistence notwithstanding, recognition of her work

as an M.D. did not extend far from her cubicle in the Patent Office. One of her patients, recovering from illness and allowed to go for a walk in uniform, was stopped on a Washington street by a guard who looked at his permission slip and said, "I shall have to place you under arrest, for here is the name of a woman on this pass and there are no women surgeons in the army." He was able to prove otherwise. (She endeared herself to the convalescent soldiers by giving out such passes to let them take walks outside the Patent Office, but had to lecture one man who delightedly showed her a pass with her name on it that he freely confessed he had forged.)

2

Ironically, although Mary probably did not know it at the time, a recent occupant of the Patent Office, locale of the Indiana Hospital, was a forty-year-old native of Oxford, Massachusetts, who kept busy proving that nurses were as valuable in wartime as physicians—maybe more so.

Clara Barton, daughter of a farmer and former soldier, was a schoolteacher who in 1854 began work as a clerk in the patent office—the first white-collar female employee of the federal government in Washington. Until 1861 she was content at her job of copying government documents in fine copperplate script but found more important and satisfying employment when the first battle casualties began arriving in the capital. She was dismissed from her clerkship for spending too much time away from her desk ministering to the wounded men of the Sixth Massachusetts Regiment, then housed in the Senate chamber, and after Bull Run became a familiar figure on

Union battlefields. She often drove a big, four-horse army wagon loaded with food and warm clothing for the soldiers, bandages and lanterns for the surgeons' tents, and issued appeals in newspaper ads calling for patriotic readers to donate such items to the Union cause. Before war's end, Barton, whose only nursing training had been caring for an invalid brother, was called the "Angel of the Battlefield," and likened to her British counterpart, Florence Nightingale, who organized a band of nurses for service in the Crimean War.*

In their service to the Union army, Clara Barton and Mary Walker both became familiar nuisances as they toiled in the army's hospitals and surgeon's tents, badgering and challenging their superiors for supplies, hygienic hospital conditions, and in general, better care for the sick and wounded. While there is no evidence that the two actually ever met, each certainly knew of the other, probably during the war and afterward.

Mary did meet, and was annoyed by, another celebrated Civil War nurse, and in a rare instance of remarking on a famous contemporary, actually left a record of the encounter.

Dorothea Dix was a social and political activist who traveled throughout the United States and Europe campaigning for better jail and penitentiary conditions and for humane treatment of the poor and insane. At age fifty-nine she volunteered

---

* After performing relief work in Europe during the Franco-Prussian War, Barton campaigned for the creation of the American Red Cross, and upon its launch in 1882 became its first president. She was present with the Red Cross at famines, earthquakes, hurricanes, floods, yellow fever epidemics, and an 1896 massacre in Armenia. At age seventy-seven, Barton went to Cuba to aid the wounded of the Spanish-American War. She died in 1912.

her services to the Union a week after the attack on Fort Sumter in April 1861. A month later, the War Department appointed her superintendent of female nurses, in charge of supervising all women nurses in the Union's army hospitals. Like Mary Walker, Dix was strong-willed, brusque, opinionated, and autocratic. She was neither impressed nor impeded by male medical superiors and War Department bureaucrats when she began appealing for women to serve as nurses in the army's Medical Bureau. She worked without pay, with only vaguely defined duties, but by war's end had recruited close to four thousand nurses to serve the Union forces.

Among her strict, arbitrary, requirements for recruits, Dix sought women thirty years old or older, preferred "plain looking and middle-aged" applicants dressed in modest black or brown skirts, wearing no hoops, jewelry, or other feminine "ornaments." She believed it "indecorous" and "unnatural" for young and attractive women to be assisting in surgeries, changing dressings, and bathing naked male bodies, whereas, apparently, older and more homely women could perform such tasks with social impunity.

She took her work among her nurses as seriously as she did her prewar crusades, preaching neatness, sobriety, order, industry, and obedience to her matronly volunteers. She cadged medical supplies, and received financing from private sources when the government refused them or was slow in providing them. She mother-henned her volunteers as they toiled in often nightmarish environments, and visited the hospitals, both in the field and in Washington, where she inspected the facilities and counseled the nurses and their patients.

In her encounter with "Dragon Dix" (as some nurses secretly called her), Mary was unimpressed. The superintendent made a tour of the Indiana Hospital in the winter of 1861 and seems to have looked askance at the pretty little woman dressed in a strange malelike attire and identified as "Dr. Walker." None of this fit Dorothea Dix's ideal and she seems to have made her feelings known by scowling at Dr. Walker and her unconventional outfit and unbelievable title. Mary later wrote that she was "somewhat amused" by Dix's shock when she spotted a patient whose bedding was in disarray and his foot exposed. Mary arranged the patient's sheets to cover his foot, and wrote later, disgustedly, "I was not able to understand . . . of what use any one can be who professes to work for a cause and then allows sham modesty to prevent them from doing little services that chance to come their way."

She was puzzled by Dix's "troubled mood when she spotted me," she said, but afterward "learned that a part of her mission was to try to keep young and good looking women out of the hospital." Mary found the superintendent's insistence on this ludicrous, another example of "sham modesty." She said she knew of a number of women "who like myself were between the ages of twenty-five and thirty that were full of patriotism and went to the front for the express purpose of rendering such assistance as was needed." Some of the volunteers told Mary that when they spoke to Dix about offering their services as nurses "she flatly ordered them to go home." Even after they assured her they were of the age she sought, "she discounted their word and they left. They were immediately thereafter employed as nurses in hospitals and proved to be efficient and worthy in all regards."

Mary's conclusion was "that bright and cheery faces in sick rooms are conducive to a convalescence . . . since the mind has such an influence in restoration of bodily ailments."

She did pay tribute to Dix's work among the insane, calling her a "good hearted woman" and advising that "This country should be grateful to her and for this lunatic asylum service her name will live."*

* Dorothea Dix, born in Maine in 1802, returned to her work among mental patients. She died in 1887.

Army of the Potomac

1

J. N. Green, the harried surgeon-in-charge at the makeshift Indiana Hospital, found Dr. Mary Walker a capable, tireless assistant, indispensable to him and his hundred or more sick and wounded patients, but he was aware that she could not stay with him. She had no income, not even the paltry $12 a month paid to nurses, but deserved the $100 to $130 monthly pay of an assistant. She slept in hospital alcoves, shared hospital rations with the patients, but unless the army granted her an assistant-surgeon appointment and the pay to go with it, she would have to move on. On November 5, 1861, Green wrote a letter to Clement A. Finley, the Union army's surgeon general, appealing for an official appointment and pay for Mary Walker. "I need and desire her assistance here for very much believing as I do that she is well qualified for the position," he said. "She is a graduate of a regular Medical College and has had a number of years' extensive experience, and comes highly recommended. If there is any way of securing to her compensation, you would confer a favor by lending your influence."

Mary made an appointment with the surgeon general and delivered Dr. Green's letter and her credentials in person. What transpired in Finley's office is unknown but it could not have been cordial. Finley, appointed by President Lincoln the previous May, was a formidable officer. He was sixty-four years old, a handsome six-footer in an impeccable blue uniform with gold-fringed epaulets, his face wreathed by neatly combed gray hair, a gray beard, and a sweeping gray mustache. He was a Pennsylvanian, an M.D. since 1818, and had been an army medical officer for forty-three years. His active service included the Black Hawk War of 1833, the Seminole War of 1838, the Mexican War of 1846–48, and garrison duty in the wilds of Kentucky, Arkansas, Missouri, Kansas, and Wisconsin.

An old army man with old ideas, he knew nothing of women physicians nor did he want to learn. He glanced at Mary Walker's documents, no doubt let his eyes roam over her peculiar choice of clothing, handed the papers back to her and said curtly that he could not grant any surgeon's or assistant-surgeon's appointment to a woman.

Mary, probably seeking advice on how to proceed with her appeal, also visited the assistant surgeon general, Robert C. Wood, and presented her letter from J. N. Green. Dr. Wood, a kindlier bureaucrat, told her if Finley had been out of the office when she presented her letters he, Wood, would have appointed her. But, he said, he could not override his boss's decision.

She returned to the hospital and resumed her work. She found some solace in her acceptance among her patients, writing that "as soon as the soldiers learned of my being a physician they were very much pleased, and whenever they felt worse in the night so that they wished to have a surgeon called I was the one that was sent for." This, she said, was a great relief to Dr. Green, who, before she joined him, was on call day and night and "was very much worn at his duties." He told her his work was "so constant that he had no time to go out into the street to take a walk to get a breath of fresh air" and she believed her assistance "no doubt prevented him also from passing away from overwork as did his predecessor."

She continued to walk the wards and tents with a hospital steward at her side who wrote down her description of the condition of each patient and the medicines and treatments she advised. New cases arrived daily in ambulances to the west sidewalk of the Patent Office building and, she said, "the surgeon in charge sent for me to come down and examine the cases so that no cases of possible smallpox might be taken up there."

Green valued her work to the end of their association, even offering her part of his $169 monthly salary. She declined this kindness. He needed the money for his wife and family, she said, "but I would be his assistant surgeon just the same as though I had been appointed."

2

Following the Union disaster at Manassas, President Lincoln appointed the thirty-four-year-old Philadelphian George Brinton McClellan (West Point, '46), to command the Army of the Potomac, gather a force, descend on Richmond, and put an end to southern resistence. An engineer and hero of the Mexican War, called "Young Napoleon" by some of his peers, McClellan seemed a good choice for high command. At the beginning of the war he led a force of Ohio volunteers and pushed back the Confederates in western Virginia, an effort that had earned him the rank of major general in the regular army. But he was cautious, excessively so, unwilling to move toward Richmond until he had a force of more than a quarter-million men under his command. And, while McClellan devised elaborate plans for a single massive action that would annihilate the rebels, his divisions were gathering, drilling, and parading in review on the commons east of the Capitol. In the meantime, Washington remained in a state of apprehension, fearing a Confederate attack.

Since she had no specific duties during the raw, rainy, winter of 1861, Mary frequently left the hospital to visit the city's defensive works, the volunteer camps and their rigged-up dispensaries and tent hospitals. On these occasions, so as not to be identified as a nurse or a "Bonnet Brigade" lady (a church and sewing-circle volunteer who collected food and made bandages for the wounded), she wore a striking homemade uniform made up of a blue officer's tunic, gold-striped trousers, a felt hat, and a green surgeon's sash. This remarkable outfit did not go unnoticed, but Mary had grown accustomed to stares and mumbles over even her ordinary "male habiliments." She wrote of taking a walk from the Patent Office and being accosted by a man who looked her over and asked her an abrupt and bothersome question. She responded by pulling a revolver from her jacket and after waving it under the man's nose, firing a shot into the ground. The stranger fled and police surrounded her. Under questioning, she presented her papers, explaining matter-of-factly that she didn't care to be spoken to in an impertinent manner, and was not detained.

Others approached her, attracted to a female in a martial uniform. These were women, often with their children clinging to their skirts, who had ventured to Washington to find lost sons and husbands who had volunteered for army service. The women, many of them destitute with no money for food or lodging, were fearful their menfolk were wounded or dead and wandered the city searching for some clue to their fate. Mary was touched by their plight and vowed to help them when she could.

3

Congress reconvened in December, its Radical Republicans—those advocating immediate emancipation of slaves and subjugation of the South—demanding an immediate advance on Manassas Junction and Richmond. They accused General McClellan of delaying and dithering, exaggerating the size of the Confederate forces, worrying about moving artillery on Virginia's marshy roads, and endlessly drilling his men, instead of devoting his time toward punishing the rebels.

McClellan, appointed by Lincoln as commander in chief of the Union army after the October retirement of General Winfield Scott, was called before a congressional committee investigating the conduct of the war. In mid-January 1862, he faced hours of hostile questions. Senators Benjamin Wade of Ohio and Zachariah Chandler of Michigan were particularly antagonistic and forced the general into a corner. Wade asked why McClellan was "refusing to attack the Confederates." McClellan answered that he needed time to prepare safe routes of retreat, whereupon Chandler said, "General, if I understand you correctly, before you strike at the rebels you want to be sure of plenty of room so that you can run in case they strike back." Later the two senators accused McClellan of "infernal, unmitigated cowardice."

Lincoln and his new secretary of war, Edwin M. Stanton, were losing their patience. Stanton, a Radical Republican himself, disliked McClellan on principle—the general was a Democrat with proslavery views—and said, referring to McClellan's elegant socializing, "The champagne and oysters on the Potomac must be stopped. . . . I will *force* this man McClellan to fight."

On January 27, 1862, the president took the unusual step of issuing General War Order Number One, a direct command for McClellan to advance against the enemy.

Even so, almost two months would pass before the march to Richmond began, the first steps in what came to be called the Peninsula Campaign.

Mary Walker read the Washington and New York papers and kept abreast of the war news, but by the time of the president's command to McClellan, she was no longer working at the Indiana Hospital. That January she thanked Dr. Green for his efforts on her behalf and returned to Oswego. Far from the miseries of the war and among the comforts of Bunker Hill Farm she rested, deciding if she wanted to resume lecturing and practicing medicine or return to the battle zone and proceed in her effort to win a surgeon's commission.

After a few days at home she traveled to New York City and enrolled at Hygeia Therapeutic College to study hydrotherapy, one of the then-popular branches of nontraditional medicine and among the oldest of the sectarian "schools" of medical thought. (Its proponents pointed out that Hippocrates, the father of medicine, used water in his treatment of cramps, convulsions, gout, and tetanus; and Galen, the second-century Greek physician, cured fevers exclusively by use of water.) The Hygeia "water-cure" school, founded in 1852, advocated the treatment of ailments not only through application of water internally and in baths, but through exercise, a strict regimen of personal hygiene, and diet, particularly of fruit and vegetables—advice subsequently adopted by the traditional medical profession.

After a single term of study, including attending clinics at Bellevue Hospital, Mary earned her certificate from Hygeia College in March 1862, and added the paper to her portfolio. After graduation she returned to Oswego to lecture and write articles on her favorite topic of dress reform plus some new material on the war and her experiences with the army, experiences that had just begun.

DISEASE, WOUNDS, AND TREATMENTS

Mary Walker's eclectic medical training and postgraduate hydrotherapy studies probably saved the lives of many of her patients. She at least insisted on hygiene and general cleanliness and was opposed to such "traditional" treatments as "cupping" (drawing blood), blistering, the use of leeches, and instant amputations. But a legion of Mary Walkers could not have stopped the awful death toll from disease during the Civil War. In the forty months of the war, on the Union side alone, 350,000 men died and most, at a margin of two-to-one over battlefield deaths, succumbed to disease. While significant Confederate records on disease have been lost, the ratio was probably about the same.

Simple filth was the prevailing factor. In the pre-Pasteur era of the 1860s, bacteria were unknown, as were the causation of disease and the importance of cleanliness. Camps and hospitals were surrounded by "sinks"—open latrines—where a variety of diseases, many of them fatal, flourished. Wounds were covered with filthy "lint"—usually rags or pieces of uniform. Surgeons operated in bloody and tissue-specked aprons, wielding unsterilized knives and saws. Inflammation was regarded as a natural phenomenon and abscesses and suppurating wounds were widely believed to be caused by airborne "pus corpuscles." Hemorrhages were controlled by packing the wound with astringents and other harmful chemicals.

Of Union disease casualties during the war, pneumonia and influenza killed an estimated 45,000 men; typhoid, 35,000; dysentery, 21,000; malaria, 10,000. Typhus, smallpox (vaccinations for which kept it from epidemic proportions), diphtheria, yellow fever, and other undiagnosed ailments accounted for hundreds of deaths while thousands died from surgical infections, including gangrene.

Soldiers on both sides of the conflict often concealed their wounds and diseases to avoid hospitalization, the prevailing attitude being that a field hospital was an avenue to death rather than recovery. James McPherson quotes data from a surgeon general's report that 14 percent of all Union wounded died of their wounds. This amazingly low number is perhaps a tribute to the resiliency of the human body more than to the medical treatments of the day.

The devastating effect of disease in the war was exhibited soon after Mary Walker left the Indiana Hospital in January 1862. Acting at last on the president's order to move his forces toward Richmond, General McClellan launched his Peninsula

Campaign in March when 100,000 Union troops were transported on 400 vessels from Washington to Fortress Monroe on the tip of the Virginia Peninsula. After battles at Yorktown, Fair Oaks, and Seven Pines, the campaign stalled at the end of May when the new Confederate commander, General Robert E. Lee, launched his own offensive and pushed McClellan's forces back to the Potomac by the end of July.

Camped in the sweltering marshlands of the Virginia Peninsula and along the swampy, flooded, Chickahominy River, McClellan's army was assailed by malaria, typhoid, and dysentery, reducing his battle-ready strength by one-third. Disease thus contributed significantly to McClellan's failure to press the advance on Richmond, added to the prolongation of the war, and resulted in his being replaced as general-in-chief.

Mary Walker's horror over the massive number of amputations performed in field hospitals during the war—an estimated thirty thousand amputated limbs in the Union army alone—was understandable, but more often than not, so was the surgical decision to amputate. Three out of four Civil War wounds were to the limbs and the worst of them were untreatable except by amputation. The culprit, more often than cannon shot and shrapnel, was the lead Minié bullet (usually .58 caliber); big, soft, and misshapen, it caused massive injury when it struck bone. As a rule, an amputation close to the body was fatal for eight out of ten cases; lower extremity amputations had a mortality rate of one in four.

More often than trauma—patients were routinely chloroformed—sepsis killed the amputee. Battlefield surgeons had yet to learn of Joseph Lister's antiseptic techniques and worked in bloody aprons, with unsterile instruments and even unwashed hands. The frequent result was gangrene and pyemia (bacteria-laden abscesses).

Fredericksburg

1

Mary Walker's failure to win a surgeon's commission in Washington, her return to Oswego, her studies at Hygeia College in New York, and her lecturing and writing removed her from the war zone for many months. At about the time she departed the capital, Union forces won significant victories in Kentucky under General George H. Thomas, an officer who would play a significant role in Mary's wartime story in the months to come.

In the "Western theater" of Tennessee, where his forces captured Fort Henry and Fort Donelson on the Cumberland River, General U. S. Grant became a sudden hero as "Unconditional Surrender" Grant for his demands on the Confederate commander there.

After initial setbacks, Grant was successful again in early April, at Shiloh, named for the small Methodist church in the battlefield of the Tennessee River. The bloodiest engagement of the war to date, Shiloh produced 3,500 dead and nearly 24,000 casualties on both sides.

Following the capture of the forts protecting New Orleans by Captain (soon to be Admiral) David Farragut's fleet, the city fell to federal troops in May.

McClellan's Peninsula Campaign ran its course in the summer, giving rise to Robert E. Lee to command all Confederate forces. In June, Major General John Pope, an engineering officer from Illinois, rose to command the Army of Virginia, and between August 29 and 31 led his 75,000 men against 54,000 Confederates at Manassas Junction, close by the battleground of the First Battle of Bull Run a year past. The southerners, led by Generals Thomas "Stonewall" Jackson and James Longstreet, defended against Pope's attacks and forced his retreat to Washington. Total casualties in the battle reached nearly twenty-five thousand with the Union bearing the brunt of them with 16,000 deaths. Pope was relieved of his command, replaced by the temporarily shelved George McClellan.

On September 17, McClellan and Major General Ambrose Burnside attacked the Confederates under Lee and Jackson at Antietam Creek, near the town of Sharpsburg, Maryland. The day-long battle, in which Lee's force was outnumbered over two to one by McClellan's 87,000 troops, resulted in a Union victory but at a huge cost to both sides: Antietam entered the history books as the bloodiest day of the war, producing 12,410 Union troops killed and wounded, and 10,700 Confederates.

Five days after Antietam, President Lincoln signed the Emancipation Proclamation, freeing slaves in the rebel states, and on November 7 removed the inert McClellan from all commands and appointed Major General Ambrose E. Burnside to head the Army of the Potomac.

2

Mary had been away from the war for eight months by November 1862, when she visited General Burnside's headquarters near Warrenton, Virginia, and the Bull Run battlefield at Manassas. Since she was never given to philosophical musings about such things, we do not know what impelled her return. She and her family, staunch Unionists and abolitionists, would soon celebrate Lincoln's Emancipation Proclamation, but the war was not going well for the North. Mary doubtlessly felt her services were needed, especially given the disquieting news of a typhoid epidemic among federal troops following the second fight at Manassas and the Antietam battle.

At Warrenton, she handed her papers to Burnside or to his aides, and while granted no official status, was welcomed as a volunteer. She found an old house where typhoid-stricken soldiers were lined up on the floor and spoke to the physician in charge. "I am all worn out. . . . For God's sake do something for them if you can," he told her. She pitched in and for a week nursed and treated soldiers in the Warrenton area field hospitals. "I frequently wrote letters for soldiers to their friends who had neither paper nor envelopes nor postage stamps, not the strength to write themselves," she said. She also searched and begged for medicines, and made forays among the civilian populace for such common but scarce items as kettles, basins, and pails in which to boil water, and rags for bandages and for bathing her fevered patients. When she could find no rags she tore her own nightdresses into foot-square bathing "towels."

She found board and lodging at Warrenton's only hotel and hoarded corn bread from the dinner table to give her patients—a welcome delicacy to those accustomed to a hardtack and water diet.

Somehow, probably from good reports of her work, she impressed General Burnside. This genial Indiana native, West Pointer, and Rhode Island resident, recognizable for his extravagant side-whiskers (the word "sideburns" is derived from his name) was a reluctant chief of the Army of the Potomac; indeed, he had twice refused the post. He believed, despite service in the Mexican War and an Apache campaign in the Southwest, that he was too inexperienced for such a responsibility. He had led a brigade at Bull Run, had some successes on the North Carolina coast, was less effective at Antietam, but became a Lincoln favorite and could not refuse the president's order to command.

Never hesitant to voice her opinions, Mary approached Burnside at Warrenton and convinced him that the men in the field hospitals there had to be moved to Washington for proper care. The general issued the order on November 15, 1862, directing "that Dr. Mary E. Walker be authorized to accompany and assist in caring for" the sick and wounded soldiers to the capital.

She later enjoyed telling the story of boarding the northbound train carrying the casualties to Washington and encountering an engineer who appeared to be confused and hesitant to get underway.

She asked the man why he didn't get the train moving.

"I have no authority," the man said.

"Then," said Mary, "I will give you orders. Start at once for

Washington. Oh, yes, I have the authority," and she waved Burnside's letter in the engineer's face.

The sick and wounded were installed in seven railcars normally used for livestock and freight, while some of the healthier patients rode on the roofs. When the train stopped at a switching station, Mary roamed from car to car, she said, "to see how my patients were, all of whom were as comfortable as they could expect." She wrote down their names and addresses, especially those "near the other shore"—dying—so she could write to their kin and notify the War Department.

One of her patients was fifty-year-old Henry Wilson, a United States congressman from Massachusetts, subsequently a senator and, in 1873, vice president in the Grant administration. While the train waited en route to Washington as the railcars were switched, Mary found that for a while "there was not an officer on board, or anybody who had any authority whatever on the train that was left except myself." After directing the engineer to proceed to Washington, she said, "I could not help suppressing a smile at the thought . . . that in reality I was then military conductor of the train that bore one of the law-makers of the nation . . . Since then it has been with some pride that I have recalled the fact that I have been the conductor of a train that conveyed the future Vice President of the United States."

Upon arriving in the capital, a crowd of well-wishers and volunteers were waiting with pails and baskets of sandwiches for the "sick train."

She had apparently returned to Burnside's headquarters in December after supervising the patient transfer, when a *New York Tribune* reporter sought her out and wrote a telling description of her: "Dressed in male habiliments with the ex-

ception of a girlish-looking straw hat, decked off with an ostrich feather, with a petite figure and feminine features, the
tout ensemble is quite engaging. Her reputation is unsullied, and
she carries herself amid the camp with a jaunty air of dignity
well calculated to receive the sincere respect of the soldiers."

3

Ambrose Burnside's command of the Army of the Potomac lasted but three months. The reluctant general, spurred
by Lincoln's anxiety to take the offensive against the Confederate capital, massed his entire force of 120,000 men and
marched east of his camp at Warrenton toward Richmond.
On November 19 the army reached the Rappahannock River,
across from the town of Fredericksburg. In the weeks that
passed while pontoon bridges were constructed by Union en-
gineers to cross the river, Robert E. Lee's Army of Northern
Virginia, 78,500 men, dug trenches and waited in their superb
high-ground defensive positions behind the town. The battle
of December 13–15, 1862, turned into a nightmarish slaugh-
ter as Burnside's Federals charged uphill again and again
against General James Longstreet's impregnable line of cannon and riflemen at Marye's Heights. Burnside finally with-
drew across the Rappahannock during the stormy night of
December 15. The Union casualties numbered over 12,700;
the Confederates about 5,300.

Burnside was relieved of command in January 1863, and
assigned to the Department of the Ohio.

Within a week of the demoralizing federal setback at
Fredericksburg, Mary Walker crossed the Rappahannock to
the battle zone. Again, she served as a walk-on volunteer, pre-

senting her papers to one of the commissioned surgeons, Dr. Preston King, who gave them a glance and welcomed her assistance. She had no official appointment but had tired of explaining that she was a medical school graduate and not a nurse or Bonnet Brigade helper. She wore the outfit she had fashioned to denote her station: the officers' blue greatcoat, trousers with gold stripes down the legs, and the green sash of a surgeon. She had cropped her curly hair and replaced her girlish straw hat with one of gold-braided felt.

At Lacy House, on a rise above Fredericksburg, she was assigned by the surgeon-in-charge to select certain "cases," see that their wounds were dressed, and prepare them for transfer to Washington. She had become adjusted to seeing the ghastly wounds of battle but remembered one particular case, a man who had a piece of his skull blown away by shrapnel from a cannon shell. "I could see the pulsation of the brain," she wrote clinically, "and when he talked I could see a movement of the same, slight though it was. He was perfectly sensible, and although I never saw him after he was taken to Washington, I learned that he lived several days."

Another who saw the horrors of the Fredericksburg aftermath at Lacy House was the forty-three-year-old Brooklyn poet Walt Whitman, whose brother George was wounded in the battle while serving with the Fifty-first New York Volunteers. Whitman crossed the Rappahannock in December 1862, climbed the hill to Lacy House, and saw "a heap of feet, legs, arms, and human fragments, cut bloody, black and blue, swelled and sickening . . ." outside the entrance. On December 26, 1862, he wrote in his diary, "Death is nothing here."

Mary supervised the transport of the casualties at the

gangway to the boats that would convey them across the Rappahannock, and made certain the stretchers were carried down the slope feetfirst since "taking them down head first would have produced pains in the head if not serious congestion of the brain . . ." During the boat trip she encountered the most poignant of all her "cases"—a Confederate drummer boy turned over to the Union side in a prisoner exchange. The boy, "not half grown," had been "wounded so severely in both of his legs that the Confederate surgeons had nicely amputated them and dressed them in the best manner possible." She found that the boy was a New Yorker, "the only child of a widowed mother," and upon reaching Washington was taken to Armory Square Hospital. There, "although perfectly sensible," she said, "yet from loss of vitality he passed away a day or two after his arrival at the hospital."

Some days later, Mary found—just how, she does not say—the mother of the boy, and wrote, "I can never forget the agonized expression of that woman's face. I did her some little favors that were in my power to do; and as she stated she could not go back to her home as her boy was gone, and that she desired to do what she could for other mothers' sons." Mary found a position for the woman, "as a nurse in the insane asylum in Washington where a number of soldiers had been sent, who from wounds, sickness and other causes had lost the proper use of their mental facilities."

In describing the Confederate surgeons as having "nicely" amputated the drummer boy's legs, Mary wrote with heavy irony. She knew little of battlefield surgery but had reached the early conclusion that the surgeons, with their bone saws and bloody aprons, were little more than butchers, needlessly sawing off limbs that could be saved. The doctors too often used the "opportunity to amputate for the purpose of their own practice, which was utterly cruel," she said.

After the war she wrote of assisting in an operation "where there was amputation of an arm where it was no more necessary than to amputate an arm that had never been injured." But, she said, "knowing that if I gave my opinion against amputation that I would be debarred from entering one of the largest hospitals in Washington, I gave antiseptics and the arm was removed." She witnessed other such "unnecessary amputations," but kept her mouth shut and assisted in the postoperative treatments.

"There were cases," she wrote, "where they [soldiers] had been wounded in the arm or leg, and in the most pitiful manner, and it was difficult for me to suppress my emotions, they would ask me if that leg would have to come off, if that arm would have to come off, telling me that the ward surgeon said it would have to come off, and that they would rather die than lose a leg or lose an arm." She said she "did not wish to be unprofessional and say anything to any other medical officer's patients that would seem like giving advice outside of a council," but added that she had "a little experience and observation regarding the inability of some of the ward surgeons to diagnose properly, and truthfully."

After one such operation she deemed unnecessary, she wrote later, "I then made up my mind that it was the last case that would ever occur if it was in my power to prevent such cruel loss of limbs." When visiting hospitals, "I made it my business, whenever I found that there were contemplated operations, and a complaint from a soldier that a decision had been made to remove a limb, I casually asked to see it, and in almost every instance I saw amputation was not only unnecessary, but to me it seemed wickedly cruel." She said she would swear such a patient not to repeat anything that she told him, "and then I would tell him that no one was obliged to submit to an amputation unless he chose to do so." She counseled soldiers awaiting amputations to protest and that if the physician insisted upon the surgery advised the patient that even "if he had never used swearing words to swear and declare that if they forced him to have an operation that he would never rest after his recovery until he had shot them dead."

Of such radical counseling, which, if found out by her superiors would have resulted in her immediate dismissal, she wrote after the war, "I need not say that secrecy regarding what I had told to the soldier was kept and that my advice was followed and that many a man today has the perfect and good use of his limbs who would not have had but for my advice, to say nothing about the millions of dollars in pensions that would have been paid."

She considered her advice her "solemn duty to the soldiers instead of carrying out etiquette towards my medical and surgical brothers."

While her patients kept her confidences, her medical colleagues undoubtedly learned of her ideas—and were not pleased.

4

The encounter with the boy and his mother also inspired her to try to help the women who came to the teeming capital desperately searching for information on fathers, husbands, and sons who had gone off to war and vanished in its turmoil.

Dr. Preston King, the senior surgeon in the battle zone, had overlooked Mary's eccentricities, including her outlandish homemade uniform and green surgeon's sash. He was impressed by her thankless work among the casualties of the Fredericksburg battle, so much so that he petitioned Secretary of War Edwin Stanton for her to receive some compensation besides a tent and rations.

While King's letter produced no compensation or commission, the surgeon was not the only witness to her tireless efforts. The *New York Tribune* reporter who had described her earlier saw her attending to the Fredericksburg wounded and wrote:

Among the unmarshalled host of camp-followers of the army, not the least noteworthy is Miss Mary E. Walker, or "Dr. Walker" as she is usually styled. She can amputate a limb with the skill of an old surgeon, and administer medicine equally well. Strange to say that, although she has frequently applied for a permanent position in the army medical corps, she has never been formally assigned to any particular duty. We will add that the lady referred to is exceedingly popular among the soldiers in the hospitals, and is undoubtedly doing much good.

The reporter's story was somewhat idealized—Mary did no amputations, for one thing—but she would have appreciated all of it (except being gathered among "camp-followers"), including the exaggerations. After all, she was not above exaggerating herself.

Washington, 1863

1

With her services in the war unrewarded by commission or pay, Mary remained in Washington most of 1863, eking out a living from her tiny medical practice, writing of her war experiences in *Sybil* magazine and speaking on them at Union League and Odd Fellow's gatherings. President Lincoln's Emancipation Proclamation, delivered on New Year's Day, 1863, declared freedom to all slaves in the states in rebellion against the Union and served as a favorite theme in the city's lecture halls.

It was a time when Washington's prostitutes were doing a record business, and all unescorted women were suspect and routinely turned away from ordinary boarding places, so early that year, with financial assistance from a women's suffrage group in the city, Mary stepped forward. She rented a house opposite Ford's Theatre, paying forty dollars a month for it and converted it into a "home for unprotected females and children." The females to be protected were "respectable" women, such as the widowed mother of the maimed drummer boy Mary had assisted, who were arriving in the city unescorted, carrying little more than their purse and a few dollars in cash, searching for a wounded or missing loved one. The Women's Relief Association on Tenth Street provided short-term accommodations for the women, a matter that pleased the Washington chief of police who proved helpful to Mary, seeing her work as assisting him with the homeless problem.

She sought out Brigadier General Edward R. S. Canby, a tough Kentuckian and veteran of the Mexican, Seminole, and southwestern Indian wars, then a staff officer in the capital, and from him was able to solicit food from the army's commissary department, as well as cots, blankets, sheets, pillowcases, and kitchenware. She next braced Major General Daniel H. Rucker, a veteran of nearly thirty years army service, now the highly efficient second-in-command of the Quartermaster's Bureau of the War Department. From this stern gentleman she asked for an ambulance and driver "to report to me each day for the purpose of going with these women to find their sick or wounded relatives." General Rucker, impressed with Mary's credentials, uniform, and guts, agreed.

She and her suffragette friends held benefits, appealed to lecture-hall audiences, to newspapers, and to wealthy and influential Washingtonians, including Mayor Richard Wallach and the wives of several of the city's eminent physicians, to raise money for the relief effort. These beginnings eventually led to the creation of several women's charitable organizations in the capital.

2

In her "Incidents Connected with the Army," Mary told a story of a mission of mercy that seems to have occurred during the period of her relief work in the capital. The story, as are virtually all the incidents she related in "Incidents," is undated (as is the manuscript itself) but probably took place either toward the end of 1862 or early in 1863.

She wrote of receiving a visit from the distraught mother of a Union officer, Lieutenant Wren.* Mrs. Wren was accompanied by her daughter-in-law, Lieutenant Wren's wife. The ladies, who had probably read newspaper accounts of Mary's efforts to aid unescorted females in the capital to find their loved ones, explained their dilemma. Wren's wife stated that she had learned that her husband was "somewhere beyond Manassas," that he had been stricken with sunstroke and had no news of him in many months. Now, their only child was deathly ill in the city and she was devastated "with the prospect of her only child dying, and her husband being in such a condition, beyond her reach, that she did not know but that he might die also." The Wren women begged Mary to "use her influence" to find the lieutenant and bring him back to Washington.

Mary was greatly affected by the story and agreed to help. Under normal circumstances, a visit to the War Department

---

* Mary identified Mrs. Wren as "the mother also of Ella Wren the actress." Ella Wren was, in fact, a well-regarded young actress in the Civil War era and had most recently performed on stage in Richmond in November 1861, at the time the newly formed Confederate States of America was holding its presidential and congressional elections.

would have been her first step in determining the whereabouts of the lieutenant. But, with the Wren child on his deathbed, time was all-important and she knew from experience that securing an appointment, even with a low-level bureaucrat, would take at least a day. She decided to bypass the department. In her account of the journey in search of Lieutenant Wren, Mary provided no details on how she managed to cross the Potomac alone, armed apparently with only her papers, found an officer of guards, explained her mission and her status with the army, and was allowed to pass through the Union lines. She wrote that she "took a train to Alexandria" and learned that Wren was recuperating in a camp about five miles from the end of the railway station.

Near the Alexandria station she discovered a "Christian Association" working among the wounded and from the volunteers borrowed a horse. "I knew it was dangerous riding through the country where both armies were skirmishing at different times," she said, "but as I was determined to go to Lieut. Wren; I was willing to run all kinds of risks to keep my word good."

Miraculously, she found Wren's camp and pleaded his family's case to the officer in command. The officer granted the lieutenant a leave of absence, arranged for an ambulance to transport him and Mary to the railroad station, and assigned a man to bring along her borrowed horse.

"I had never seen the man [Wren] before," Mary wrote, "and when I first saw him at the camp he was in a very despondent condition of mind, but finally, when he found what my mission was his countenance lighted up and, although he was suffering, he was so elated with the idea of going to his family that the clouds soon dispersed, and brought a beautiful sunshine to his face."

Wren was still quite sick, probably weakened by malaria as well as the aftermath of sunstroke, as the two rode in a candlelit boxcar, where Mary made a bed for him and held his head on a pillow during the train ride to Alexandria. Once there, she and her patient were placed in an ambulance and conveyed by boat to Washington's Seventh Street wharf.

She managed to get Wren on a streetcar and to K Street near the home taken by his wife and mother, and with the help of the conductor and a stranger, escorted the lieutenant to the house.

The story had a happy ending, tersely told by Mary in her memoir: "I need not express the delight felt by all parties upon the lieutenant's arrival home. His child did recover, and at the expiration of Lieutenant Wren's leave he returned to his command."

3

In the spring of 1863, Mary met President and Mrs. Lincoln at a White House reception. She said the president was "cordial," Mary Todd Lincoln "well-proportioned, fair, round-faced, lively and pleasing." She saw "Father Lincoln," as she called him, again, after the battle of Chancellorsville from May 2 to 4, where, ten miles west of Fredericksburg, Joseph "Fighting Joe" Hooker, Ambrose Burnside's replacement as general-in-chief of the Army of the Potomac, led 75,000 men in a humiliating setback. Hooker's army, arrayed against Lee's 60,000 troops and the brilliant generalship of Thomas J. Jackson, was forced to retreat after losing 17,000 casualties against Lee's 13,000. (The battle produced a setback for the Confederacy as well: "Stonewall" Jackson, accidentally shot by his own men in the failing light of May 2, had his left arm amputated after the battle and died on May 10.)

Mary recalled observing President Lincoln on May 4 at Washington's Sixth Street wharf where the president waited "for signs of Hooker's success" as Confederate prisoners taken after the battle were being conveyed across the Potomac. She saw drops of perspiration rolling down the president's "careworn cheeks" on that hot and melancholy occasion.

In Washington, on June 23, 1863, Mary had an unhappy encounter with another Lincoln, no relation to the president. She visited the Thirty-fourth New York Volunteers' headquarters of Colonel William Slosson Lincoln, a fifty-year-old New Yorker, lawyer, and postwar Republican congressman. Mary's visit was on behalf of a sick soldier, probably one whose mother or wife was among those housed with the Women's Relief Association on Tenth Street. She appealed to Lincoln to grant the soldier a furlough and Lincoln refused the request.

When their brief meeting ended she said, "Well, Colonel, I thank you for your frankness, but I see in this case you will force me to appeal to those of higher rank." To this he replied with an abundance of sarcasm, "How I shall regret that, my dear doctor. To have it said, that a *lady* had been *forced* to anything by an officer of the 34th would mortify the whole command."

After her departure, Colonel Lincoln wrote of Dr. Walker's

quasi-military outfit as "hermaphrodite-rigged" with a "close-buttoned, blue cloth frock, the skirts falling to her knees; tight-fitting black pants and congress boots."

Mary, by now no stranger to officers and their rejections, dismissed them and their petty ideas: "Woman's mind is an emanation from Deity, and man's mind is very probably emanated from the same source," she wrote, "and the difference in the minds of the sexes is owing in part to the roughness of the clay. . . ."

Meantime, the war was passing her by. In May 1863, General U. S. Grant's campaign around Vicksburg, Mississippi, resulted in capture of the river and cutting the Confederacy in half; and in the first three days of July, the Gettysburg battle produced a staggering butcher's bill (of 85,000 Union forces, 23,000 killed, wounded, or missing; of 70,000 Confederates, 20,000 casualties), but ended all southern attempts to advance on Washington.

Then, from September 19 to 21, the three-day battle near Chickamauga Creek, just across the Georgia border of Tennessee, produced a Confederate victory and another 16,000 Union casualties (18,500 among the southern forces) and also gave prominence to an extraordinary Union officer.

This was General George Henry Thomas, a West Pointer, veteran of the Mexican and Seminole wars, a brilliant commander beloved by his troops (who called him "Pap"), modest and disdainful of personal glory. He was a native of Southampton, Virginia, who remained loyal to the Union when the Civil War broke out, for which loyalty his family disowned him and his lands and home were confiscated by his native state. (Even after the war, when his sisters were in need, they rejected his offers of assistance and remained alienated).

He was a forty-six-year-old brigadier general of the Army of the Cumberland when, at Chickamauga, after most of the army had fled the field, he stubbornly held out at a place called Snodgrass Hill, saving the army from destruction and earning the nickname the "Rock of Chickamauga."

General Thomas, who knew something about rejection, would become something of a champion of Mary Edwards Walker.

4

On November 2, 1863, Mary wrote to Secretary of War Edwin Stanton for permission to raise a regiment of men to be called "Walker's U.S. Patriots," of which she would serve as "first Assistant Surgeon." She said, "Having been so long the friend of soldiers . . . I feel confident that I can be successful in getting reenlistment of men who would not enlist in any other person's Reg.," and offered the novel idea that some of the volunteers might be prison parolees.

Not surprisingly, the idea was rejected, although Stanton did pay homage to her militant spirit.

She took a different tack on January 11, 1864, in a letter to "His Excellency," President Lincoln. She wrote to ask him to intervene in her case, since she had been denied a commission "solely on the ground of sex," when her services "have been tested and appreciated without a commission and without compensation." She asked to be assigned to duty at Douglas Hospital, one of the eighty-odd hospitals created in the city in wartime, "in the female ward, as there cannot possibly be any objection urged on account of sex."

Addressing the president in the third person, she said she would:

> . . . much prefer to have an extra surgeon's commission with orders to go wherever there is a battle that she may render aid in the field hospitals, where her energy, enthusiasm, professional abilities, and patriotism will be of the greatest service in inspiring the true soldier never to yield to traitors, and in attending the wounded brave. She will not shrink from duties under shot and shells, believing that her life is of no value in the country's greatest peril if by its loss the interests of future generations shall be promoted.

Lincoln replied that he could not personally interfere in the Medical Department of the army, "an organized system in the hands of men supposed to be learned in that profession." He said that "it would injure the service for me, with strong hand, to thrust among them anyone, male or female, against their consent." He added that if the service were willing to have Dr. Walker in charge of a female ward, he would also be willing "but I am sure controversy on the subject would not subserve the public interest."

Mary, forever unwilling to take no for an answer, even from the president, kept busy. Somehow, probably through her contacts in Washington, she identified Illinois Congressman John Franklin Farnsworth as friendly to her efforts. He had served as a brigadier general of the Illinois volunteer cavalry at the beginning of the war and had resigned in 1863 to take up a seat in the Thirty-eighth Congress. He wrote a letter on her behalf, addressed to Assistant Surgeon General Robert C. Wood, who had demonstrated some sympathy for Mary's cause during her service in the Indiana Hospital in the winter of 1861. "She has been for more than two years past active, efficient, and very useful in her ministrations to the sick and wounded," Farnsworth wrote, adding, "I hope you will give her some good position where she can properly support herself, and at the same time, be most useful."

She also appears to have badgered War Secretary Stanton at about this time, asking to be assigned to someplace in the war zone where she could "be most useful," the result of which was Stanton's authorizing her to report to the surgeon-in-charge of the Army of the Tennessee in Chattanooga.

Tennessee

There is no precise record of Mary Walker's arrival in Tennessee—how she traveled, when she got there, or to whom she reported. By some accounts, she reached Chattanooga in the fall of 1863, a month or so after the Chickamauga battle of September 19 to 21, and worked among the thousands of Federal casualties produced by the fight. Other researchers place her advent at the headquarters of the Army of the Tennessee after the Chattanooga campaign in the winter of 1863.

Since it appears she was still in Washington in January 1864, when she appealed to President Lincoln for a "surgeon's commission with orders to go wherever there is a battle," she probably reached Tennessee the following month, February 1864.

There is also varying information on why she was sent to Tennessee and who approved the mission. According to one account, Secretary of War Edwin Stanton authorized her to report to General William T. Sherman, commander of the Army of the Tennessee, and sent a message to Sherman requesting that he assign her to a field hospital. Another version is that she was dispatched to Tennessee to report to Union medical authorities at Chattanooga, where her credentials as a physician would be examined and evaluated before any assignment was given to her. Why such an evaluation could not have been made in Washington is unknown, unless Mary had cajoled Stanton to send her to Tennessee and the secretary had agreed, providing she would assent to the evaluation once she got there.

In any event, she reached Chattanooga early in 1864, at a time when Sherman was taking over command of the western armies and preparing to launch his Atlanta campaign. On March 8 she appeared before a board of medical officers of the Army of the Cumberland* to undergo the examination of her credentials.

She again presented her papers: her medical degree from Syracuse Medical College, her graduate certificate from Hygeia Therapeutic College, the recent letters of recommendation from Congressman Farnworth and Assistant Surgeon General Dr. Robert C. Wood, and the older letters from Dr. J. N. Green of the Indiana Hospital and Dr. Preston King, the senior surgeon at Fredericksburg.

---

* The Army of the Cumberland, commanded by General George Thomas in 1864, numbered 70,000 men. It is not to be confused with the Army of the Tennessee, a different unit, commanded by General W. T. Sherman at the time of Mary Walker's appearance in Chattanooga.

There are two versions of what transpired before this board, but, with the exception of a differing name or two, the outcome was the same: a humiliating experience for Mary Walker.

One version has a Dr. Perin as the medical director for the Army of the Cumberland perusing her paperwork, looking up at the tiny, strangely dressed woman, declaring her "a medical monstrosity," and ordering her to be questioned by a board of army physicians. These unnamed men determined her to be so inadequate "as to render it doubtful whether she has pursued the study of medicine." The examiners conceded that she knew something of obstetrics—scarcely a recommendation for a battlefield surgeon's post—but her knowledge of disease and remedies, they said, was negligible.

Mary later denied any such examination took place before Dr. Perin, but said she *was* examined by a Dr. [George E.] Cooper and his medical officers and maintained that, "I stood my ground and told him I would go to Gen'l [George] Thomas and report him if he did not assign me to duty without any more insult."

She said Cooper treated her with disdain from the moment she met him and heard him inform her he did not want any "female surgeons" in his command.

"I had scarcely entered the room before I felt the Cooper influence and was almost dumb. I felt that the examination was intended to be a farce," she wrote President Andrew Johnson in September 1865, "& more than half the time was consumed in questions regarding subjects that were exclusively feminine and had no sort of relations to the diseases & wounds of soldiers."

Dr. Roberts Bartholomew, one of her examiners on the Perin (or Cooper) board, wrote in a New York medical journal after the war that she was "dressed in that hybrid costume," and,

> ... betrayed such utter ignorance of any subject in the whole range of medical science, that we found it a difficult matter to conduct an examination. The Board unanimously reported that she had no more medical knowledge than an ordinary housewife, that she was, of course, entirely unfit for the position of medical officer, and that she might be made useful as a nurse.

All her examiners, whether Perin, Cooper, or Bartholomew, and all the hierarchy of the surgeon general's office in the capital, were, of course, traditional allopaths, medicos instantly disdainful of "unorthodox" practitioners like Mary Walker. Her Syracuse College diploma told them she was an "eclectic," the Hygeia College certificate meant she favored water treatments and such arcane ideas as personal hygiene and cleanliness. These traditionals would have shaken their heads in disbelief at her bizarre opposition to such treatments as massive uses of purgatives and her disdain of surgery, which at the time consisted chiefly of amputations.

In brief, whether spoken aloud or not, these superior officers dismissed Mary Walker as a quack.

She did not betray her real emotions at the rude dismissal of the medical board—she rarely displayed such feelings in her writings. Still, while she said, "I stood my ground," she was hurt by the whole affair and righteously angry.

The medical men thought that waving Mary away would discourage her, but even such a formidable figure as General William Tecumseh Sherman tried that tack and failed.

According to an article in *The New York Times* dated September 21, 1869, she appeared before Sherman at some point in her Tennessee service to complain, "The men are making unseemly remarks about my attire."

"Then why don't you wear a dress?" the irascible general asked.

"The male attire is more practical for my work," she said.

While there is no record that Sherman did anything about her complaint, he could not argue her pointed reply.

Mary had warned Dr. Cooper that if he did not assign her to duty "without any more insult," she would report to his superior officer, General George Thomas, and did so after Cooper and his naysaying board rejected her. She appears to have met the "Rock of Chickamauga" early upon her arrival in Chattanooga, probably by introducing herself at his headquarters (she was never shy in approaching the eminent, from the president of the United States on down) and found him sympathetic, so much so that he became her "noble general" ever afterward.

The handsome Thomas, forty-seven years old, steely-eyed and gray-bearded, had taken command of the Army of the Cumberland in October 1863. He was battle-tested from his service as an artillery officer in Mexico, Florida, the Indian frontier of Texas, and in the present war, and had genuine concern for his men, whether in fighting trim or as casualties. He established the war's most efficient hospital service, where the use of chloroform in surgical tents was a standard practice, and had railroad cars reconstructed to serve as field hospitals, a mobile system that saved countless lives, Union and Confederate, in the Chickamauga and Chattanooga battles.

And, as it turned out, General Thomas hired the first female doctor in the Union army.

Mary probably heard of Thomas's mobile hospital innovations when she came calling and the scene had to be memorable. Thomas was a huge man, over six feet tall and weighing two hundred pounds, while his caller was a foot shorter and a hundred pounds lighter. To her amazement she learned that for once her timing was impeccable. The assistant surgeon of the Fifty-second Ohio Volunteers of the Army of the Cumberland had died in January 1864, and General Thomas, to Mary's everlasting gratitude, was impressed by her papers and prior service. He ignored the findings of his own board of medical officers and appointed her civilian contract surgeon to the Fifty-second Ohio, headquartered at Gordon's Mill near Chattanooga.

Mary's luck held out when she reported for duty and met the commanding officer of the Fifty-second, Brigadier General Daniel McCook Jr., a prewar law partner of W. T. Sherman. A native of Carrollton, Ohio, the tall and lean McCook was a member of a distinguished, and tragic, family of Civil War officers. Two of his brothers, Alexander and Robert, were Union generals, as was a cousin, Edward. Robert had been killed by Confederate partisans in Tennessee the previous August and Daniel himself did not have long to live: He would be killed on the heights of Kennesaw Mountain, Georgia, on June 27 of that year.

When Mary met Daniel McCook in the spring of 1864, the two had an Ohio connection, which Mary no doubt mentioned (she had launched her medical career in Columbus in 1855) and the thirty-four-year-old general welcomed her and authorized his quartermaster to assign her a horse and saddle. She later referred to McCook as "a man of great sympathy and a large sense of justice" and said he once asked her to "review the vedettes in his absence." She added a red officer's sash to her uniform and inspected the sentries as ordered. "This is the only instance in the war as far as I am aware, where a woman made a revue," she wrote.

As a civilian contract surgeon she held no commission or military rank, but at least was entered on the paymaster's books to receive the pay equivalent of a first lieutenant, just under one hundred dollars a month. Her billet was a "sleeping room" in the kitchen of a miller's house.

With her assortment of medicines, scissors, probes, scalpels, and hemostats, and with two revolvers in her saddlebags, she began making daily trips on horseback through the picket lines to attend the sick and wounded, soldier and civilian, in war-ravaged Chattanooga and beyond. She crossed enemy lines to assist women and children, frequently sick and near death, living in the Georgia settlements and at the mercy of foraging parties and lawless bands preying on the populace. She performed simple surgeries, pulled teeth, in one case lanced a "frog felon" (probably an ingrown toenail), delivered babies, treated typhoid victims, and used supplies taken from Federal stores to feed and treat her patients.

"The people, while they were grateful for the services rendered, were in the greatest of financial distress," she recalled.

"In but one case did I take a fee and then it was a five dollar greenback that was so urged upon me in an obstetrical case that I received it."

The entire Tennessee-Georgia border country was in a pitiable condition, she said. "Both armies had been upon the ground . . . but the Confederate army had been all through there pressing every man into service, even those that were too young . . . and it left the women, as they said, 'To root hog or die.' . . . I cannot tell you how sincerely I pitied those people."

Later she would describe these experiences to justify her award of the Medal of Honor: "The special valor," she said somewhat grandly, "was for going into the enemy's ground, when the inhabitants were suffering for professional service, and sent to our lines to beg for assistance; and no man surgeon was willing to respond for fear of being taken prisoner and by my doing so the people were won over to the Union."

Thirty-six years after her service with McCook's regiment, Rev. Nixon B. Stewart, chaplain of the Fifty-second Ohio, wrote of Mary Walker in a regimental history: "She began to practice in her profession among the citizens in the surrounding country. Every day she would pass out of the picket line, attending the sick. . . . How she got her commission no one seemed to know. . . . She wore curls, so that everybody would know she was a woman." He described her as slender and frail-looking and also stated, "Many of the boys [of the Fifty-second Regiment] believed her to be a spy."

Rev. Stewart, who as late as 1900 was still upset at the idea of a female physician in his midst, said, in a caustic contradiction of the facts: "The men seemed to hate her and she did little or nothing for the sick of the regiment. . . . We thought of our mothers and sisters as our dearest friends and could not bear the thought of having them share with us the rude usages of camp life."

In the meantime, Mary's special nemesis, Dr. George E. Cooper, reported to the surgeon general in Washington that Mary E. Walker "is useless, ignorant, trifling and a consummate bore & I cannot imagine how she ever had a contract made with her as Actg. Asst. Surgeon."

That she had no such contract and was serving as a uncommissioned civilian contract surgeon was not of concern to Cooper. He simply could not entertain the idea that a trifling, boring person with nontraditional medical training might do useful medical work.

And a woman?

Impossible.

Spy

1

While she was often accompanied by an orderly and even an officer or two when attending to patients at field hospitals within the Union lines, on occasion Mary rode alone into the countryside "where there was great distress" among the southern civilians in the war zone. There, she said, were "people not only suffering for food but for medical assistance." General McCook gave her unusual latitude in ministering to these farm folk, a fact Mary said was attributable to his "great sympathy and large sense of justice."

While the civilians she treated were appreciative, they were wary: None had seen a female doctor before, certainly not one in male dress, and in a Union uniform at that. She recounted one venture beyond the lines when she extracted a tooth from the wife of a Colonel Gordon "who was himself a long distance away in the Confederate army. . . . Much to the relief of the suffering, I drew the wicked tooth away in triumph," she wrote. On another mission away from camp, when she was forced to stay overnight at a patient's home, the family informed her she could not sleep in the same room as their daughter. When she questioned this, Mary was informed that the people in the vicinity thought she was a man "because no woman could know as much as I knew."

She had to borrow a dress and bonnet to ride into the settlement of Ringgold, just across the Georgia border below Chattanooga, to buy some thread for the young daughter of the family she was treating. She borrowed the dress, rolled her trousers up under it and, with the daughter, rode in a wagon to Ringgold. She purchased five dollars worth of thread, then startled the clerk by offering him a greenback "because the Confederate money was so depreciated that it was not worth half its original value." The clerk took the money but on the return trip Mary had a close call with a Confederate patrol. As their buggy was ascending a steep hill, two officers rode up to question them. Mary did not fear being taken prisoner but she said, "I had a greater fear for both myself and herself in that lonely place," apparently referring to a fear of being physically assaulted. While Mary did not climb down from the carriage, fearing the men would see the trousers under her skirt, her young companion explained to the officers the thread-buying trip into Ringgold, and were permitted to proceed.

Mary was convinced that General McCook's humane treatment of the sick and starving civilians in the Gordon's Mill vicinity, including the refugees who came through the Fifty-second Ohio lines, and her work among them, "caused a great many of them to abandon their allegiance to the confederacy."

2

When making her rounds in the countryside unaccompanied, Mary left her revolvers behind to ensure that she would be treated as a noncombatant if captured by a Confederate patrol. On April 10, 1864, two months after her assignment to the Fifty-second Ohio Volunteers, this was precisely what happened. She rode out of camp alone, took a wrong road just south of the Georgia-Tennessee border, encountered a Confederate sentry, threw up her hands, declared that she was unarmed, and was taken prisoner.

Details of her capture and subsequent imprisonment are sketchy. Mary, the best source for her experiences, was mysteriously tentative in writing about them. Mercedes Graf, in her study of Mary Walker's Civil War years, states, "In postwar years, her military exploits were among Walker's favorite lecture topics. Therefore, it seemed surprising that she never wrote about the prison experiences that followed her capture." Indeed, Mary's "explanation" for this void in her postwar lectures and diary entries, defies belief. Of questions asked of her imprisonment, she said, "To answer such inquiries in detail, repeated as they are a thousand times, would engross all my time, and prove an exhausting task."

In fact, her silence on the events between April 10 and August 12, 1864, is due to the fact that she was on a spying mission when taken prisoner. While her work was low level, reporting any troop movements she observed while on the fringes of the Confederate lines in Georgia, she took the work seriously and abided by its code of secrecy.

Mary's "noble Gen'l," George H. Thomas, substantiated this role when he wrote later, "She desired to be sent to the

52nd Ohio as Acting Assistant Surgeon, so that she might get through our lines and get information of the enemy. I consented to let her go and she was soon afterwards captured."

(Thomas's recollection is the probable source for the entry on Mary Walker in the 1936 *Dictionary of American Biography:* "For the first three years of the Civil War she was a nurse [sic] in the Union Army. Between March and August 1864, she appears to have served as a spy while nominally attached to the 52nd Ohio Infantry in the capacity of contract surgeon.")

While she did not speak publicly or publish writings on the subject, the evidence of her role as spy is seen repeatedly in her private correspondence. For example, after her release from captivity, she wrote to Secretary of War Stanton offering her services again and referring to her Confederate prison experience: ". . . to give you information as to their forces and plans and any important information." She wrote of a "Mr. Allen of the 'Secret Service'" wishing her to cross the enemy lines as "a common lady, with no medical pretensions, & wear long dresses & hoops." She said she told Mr. Allen she would need a hundred dollars to buy three such outfits as she "had scarcely an article that could be worn in that style," but he could not give her the money. (Mary could not resist adding her idea of the utmost proof of her patriotism: "I wear the Bloomer costume and nothing but the good of my Country would induce me to wear the unphysiological fashionable dress.")

The Stanton letter is particularly remarkable in that the "Mr. Allen of the 'Secret Service'" was undoubtedly the renowned detective Allen Pinkerton, who traveled and performed his investigative work in Tennessee, Georgia, and

Mississippi, under the name "E. J. Allen." In 1861, while investigating a railway case, Pinkerton discovered a plot against Abraham Lincoln in which a group of conspirators intended to assassinate the president-elect in Baltimore during a stopover en route to Washington and his inauguration. Pinkerton was able to warn Lincoln of the plot, and the president-elect's itinerary was changed. Lincoln later hired Pinkerton to organize a "secret service" to obtain military information in the southern states during the Civil War.

An example of the general knowledge of Mary's service as a spy surfaced in 1876, when her application for a disability pension was denied. The commissioner of the Pension Office wrote, ". . . your appointment as contract surgeon was made for the purpose, not of performing of duties pertaining to such office, but that you might be captured by the enemy to enable you to obtain information concerning their military affairs; in other words, you were to act in the role of a spy for the United States military authorities."

While she was alone as a female physician-spy for the Union, female nurse-spies were familiar on both sides of the war. The best known of these on the Union side was Sara Edmonds, of New Brunswick, Canada, who, like Mary, often dressed as a male. Edmonds, however, carried her disguise to the extreme: She adopted the name Frank Thompson and enlisted in the Second Michigan Infantry in 1861. She took part in the First Battle of Bull Run, spied among the Confederates at Chickahominy, Virginia, and in General Joseph E. Johnston's camps near Richmond. She also nursed the wounded in and around the battlefields of Virginia and in 1865 wrote a book about her experiences, *Nurse and Spy in the Union Army,* which sold 175,000 copies, the profits from which she donated to war relief efforts.

Mary Walker's idea that she might be useful as a spy actually appears to have predated her arrival in Tennessee. Evidence exists that as early as November 1862, when she arrived at General Ambrose Burnside's headquarters near Warrenton, Virginia, she suggested to the general that she could use her status as a physician to gather information inside the enemy lines. Burnside was not interested in the idea. Then, after the Chancellorsville battle, she is a said to have presented her case to Generals Darius Couch and Winfield Scott Hancock of the Army of the Potomac and found them sympathetic. Their commander, General George Meade, however, was not, and until she reported to the Gordon's Mill camp in Tennessee, nothing came of her plan.

However it came together, there is ample testimony of the espionage—some of it from Mary herself, who most often kept mum on the subject—which led to her being taken prisoner in northwestern Georgia on April 10, 1864.

Castle Thunder

1

News of her capture was dispatched to the *Richmond Inquirer* by its correspondent with Confederate forces on the Tennessee-Georgia border, and it appeared in the paper on April 14. The dispatch gave no hint that she was taken prisoner as a spy and provided Mary's excuse for wandering into the southern lines: "Miss Mary E. Walker, Assistant-surgeon of the Fifty-second Ohio, was captured by pickets and brought here yesterday," the article stated. "She is quite sprightly, converses fluently, says she only wished to deliver letters and had no idea of being arrested."

Her captors delivered her to Lieutenant General Daniel Harvey Hill, who commanded the Confederate forces in the area (and, incidentally, was a brother-in-law of Thomas "Stonewall" Jackson). This officer, who had been in the thick of the battles at Chickamauga and Chattanooga, took no interest in the female physician and ordered her sent to Richmond as a prisoner. Before this was accomplished, however, it appears she spent a month at the headquarters of General Joseph E. Johnston, commander of the Confederate Army of Tennessee, near Dalton, Georgia, twenty miles south of Chattanooga. There, according to biographer Charles Snyder, "being cooperative and friendly she was permitted to treat a limited number of patients."

In May 1864, Mary was taken by rail the seven hundred miles from Dalton to Richmond, Virginia, where a Confederate commissary captain named Benedict J. Semmes, a onetime wholesale grocer in Memphis, saw her disembark. In his description of the moment, skewed by his hatred of all things Yankee, he said that the crowd at the rail station were "both amused and disgusted" at what he called "the sight of a *thing* that nothing but the debased and depraved Yankee nation could produce—'a female doctor'—brought in by the pickets this morning." He said she was dressed in "the full uniform of a Federal surgeon, looks, hat & all, & wore a cloak"; observed that she was "not good looking and of course had tongue enough for a regiment of men"; and offered the opinion that she would have been at home in a lunatic asylum.

For such a foe of tobacco, one who lectured that it caused lassitude, irritability, defective memory, paralysis, and insanity, one who in later life was known to knock a pipe or cigar from a man's mouth with an umbrella she carried for that purpose, Mary's place of confinement in Richmond, a filthy and verminous former tobacco factory and warehouse, was particularly ironic.

It was called Castle Thunder, a dramatic name invented by its commandant, Captain George W. Alexander, CSA, "to be a terror to evil-doers," and stood on Cary Street, facing the dock and the river. Nearby, the better-known Libby Prison, which occupied the buildings of a former ship chandler company, housed at capacity 1,200 prisoners. By comparison, Castle Thunder comprised three three-storied brick buildings and held 1,400 prisoners (though it eventually housed 3,000). The inmates were segregated by sex, race, and offense, and included a number of "Unionists"—political prisoners—plus Confederate deserters, various cutthroats and common prostitutes, "the refuse of the southern army," a Richmond newspaper said. Also numbered among the incarcerated were perceived spies, such as Mary Walker, and professional spies, including some captured Pinkerton Detective Agency operatives.

While less a death camp than the Andersonville stockade in southwest Georgia, Castle Thunder was still a hellhole: overcrowded, overrun with rats and insects, without sanitation facilities, and disease-ridden. Its inmates suffered from all manner of illness, ranging from pneumonia to nameless fevers and malnutrition. Of the latter, a twenty-nine-year-old prisoner named Robert Sneden of the Fortieth New York Volunteers claimed that the *Richmond Inquirer* "daily advocates starving us, so that we cannot run away." Sneden spent a brief time at Castle Thunder before he was sent south to Andersonville in early 1864.

Captain Alexander, a Pennsylvanian and former naval officer, kept a "taut ship," running his prison like a Confederate Captain Bligh, having unruly prisoners flogged with cat-o'-nine-tails, stringing them up by the thumbs to an overhead beam with their toes barely touching the ground, and chaining the worst of them in solitary cells on bread and water diets.

He was a feared and formidable figure, remembered as riding at full gallop on his black horse along Richmond's streets with a huge, black Bavarian boar hound named Nero following at his heels. The dog regularly patrolled Castle Thunder and was described as "ordinarily good natured, playful, and docile, but when angered or provoked was terrible looking, and dangerous." Alexander himself seemed to fear Nero, keeping him at bay with a horsewhip and cocked revolver which he would occasionally fire over the animal's head.*

2

Richmond's newspapers were agog at the capture of the "female Yankee surgeon." On April 22, the *Richmond Sentinel* devoted front-page space to Mary, attending especially to "her appearance on the street in full male costume, with the exception of a gipsy hat," which the paper said,

> . . . created quite an excitement amongst the idle negroes and boys who followed and surrounded her. She gave her name as Dr. Mary E. Walker, and declared that she had been captured on neutral ground. She was dressed in black pants and black or dark talma or paletot [a close-fitting jacket]. She was consigned to the female ward of Castle Thunder, there being no accommodations at the Libby for prisoners of her sex.

---

* Alexander later faced a court of inquiry on charges that he "received greenbacks from prisoners in consideration that he would endeavor to have them discharged." He was suspended from his duties but was cleared of the accusations. He died in 1895.

The reporter betrayed any tradition of southern gentility in ending his story, "We must not omit to add that she is ugly and skinny, and apparently above thirty years of age."

The Richmond Whig seems to have had the same news source on Mary's appearance in also reporting in a page-one story on April 22 that the female Yankee surgeon who was recently captured

> . . . is about thirty years old and quite ugly, but has an intelligent appearance and a pleasant voice. She was dressed in male costume—black pants, fitting tight, a jacket and short talma of black or dark blue cloth, but wore a dark straw Gipsy hat, that might be construed as announcing her sex. She gave her name as Dr. Mary E. Walker, of the Union army, and said she was a regular allopathic physician. As she passed through the streets in charge of a detective, her unique appearance attracted unusual attention, and an immense crowd of negroes and idlers formed for her a volunteer escort to Castle Thunder.

(If she did in fact claim to be "a regular allopathic physician," she did so to avoid another round of distressing questions about her credentials.)

No matter what was said of her, Mary did not require newspaper coverage to make her presence known. She ate the same meager meals of corn bread, rice, peas, and bacon as the other prisoners, but did not hesitate to complain to the commandant and guards of the often disgusting rations of maggoty rice and moldy bread (which she said she often fed to the rats). She spoke out on the filth and vermin, the straw mattresses and ragged blankets, insisted that fresh vegetables be added to the menu to ward off scurvy, and in general made a Yankee nuisance of herself.

Since she carried papers identifying her as a contract surgeon attached to the Fifty-second Ohio Regiment, and perhaps because of her nagging demands, she was given a private room and permitted certain privileges. The Castle Thunder chaplain, Reverend J. L. Burrows, said she "was sometimes permitted to stroll into the streets, where her display of Bloomer costume, blouse, trousers and boots secured her a following of astonished and admiring boys." He added that "She is quite chatty, and seemed rather to enjoy the notoriety of her position."

The *Sentinel,* on May 2, 1864, took notice of one of her strolls—and again of her "costume":

> Some excitement among the juveniles and negroes was produced Saturday morning, by the appearance on the streets of Mary E. Walker, the Yankee surgeon, in her outré costume, of men's pants, boots and short cloak and broad brimmed beaver hat. She was walking between two detectives, who conducted her to Gen. Winder's office, and thence back to the Castle. The cause of her visit to the General we did not learn.

(General John H. Winder was then the provost marshal of Richmond, responsible for military discipline in the Richmond area, counterespionage, the defense of the city, and the administration of prisoners of war.)

On the same date *The Richmond Whig* offered a possible reason for her visit with the general while adding to its habit of maligning her: "This disgusting production of Yankee land was marched from Castle Thunder to Gen. Winder's office Saturday morning to the very great amusement of crowds of negroes, male and female, and many white boys," the story ran. "We did not hear the object of her visit to headquarters, but presume it had something to do with her being sent North. She is still dressed in male attire, which begins to look the worse for wear."

Mary had quickly become a favorite source for news items in Richmond's newspapers. Not to be outdone by the *Sentinel* and *Whig*, the *Examiner*, Richmond's premier scandal sheet, on May 13, 1864, accused her of spending her confinement "not in reading medical works on saw bones and the treatment of camp itch" but on "devouring all the novel nonsense and trash she can get hold of with a negro character in them." The reporter also said she refused to quit her Bloomer style of dress and find one "more becoming to her sex." A month later the *Examiner* tested the limits of press idiocy and the gullibility of its readers in reporting on June 29, 1864, that Mary Walker "is now lady and lioness of all she surveys. Sometimes she exhibits herself in costume on the balcony of the Castle. It is said she has a Yankee Major lover among the prisoners at the Libby prison, which is one square below the Castle, and within easy signal range."

But for all the slanders and malignities of the Richmond press, the issue of her manner of dress rankled Mary more than accusations that she was ugly and disgusting. At least once she tried to respond to the incessant reportage on her "costume," writing to another of the city's papers: "Sir, Will you please correct the statement made in this morning's *Dispatch* in regard to my being 'dressed in male attire,' as such is not the case. Simple justice demands correction. I am attired in what is usually called the 'Bloomer' or 'Reform Dress,' which is similar to all ladies' [attire] with the exception of its being shorter and more physiological than long dresses."

Because of the chronic shortage of medical personnel at Castle Thunder, Mary appears to have treated some prisoners there, services which may account for her private room and "certain privileges," but these duties were short-lived. In July, after two months incarceration, she fell ill, plagued by an eye infection and "physical and emotional distress," and began petitioning for her freedom.

The *Richmond Enquirer* on June 10, 1864, exactly two months after her capture, reported under the heading **WANTS TO GO HOME**: "Dr. Mary E. Walker, Assistant Surgeon, U. S. A., 52d Ohio Volunteers, captured in Georgia, is very tired of her captivity in Castle Thunder. She wants to go home. . . . Sensible female."

On June 29, the *Examiner* followed its custom of inventing news. **MISS WALKER, THE YANKEE SURGEONESS**, its headline ran, followed crazily by "Miss Doctress, Miscegenation, Philosophical Walker, who has so long ensconced herself very quietly in Castle Thunder, has loomed into activity again." The reporter claimed that Mary had recently "got mad, pitched into several of her room-mates in long clothes, and tore out handfuls of auburn hair from the head of one of them," then "proclaimed secession, and went into another apartment, where she is now lady and lioness of all she surveys. Sometimes she exhibits herself in costume on the balcony of the Castle, or walks in the garden below. . . . she thinks it hard, very hard, that she is not allowed to go home."

Not until late July was Mary able to place her appeal to be released before Brigadier General William Montgomery Gardner, commander of all Confederate military prisons east of the Mississippi and the new provost marshal of Richmond. On July 26, the *Whig* provided a hint that Mary might have been released earlier but for certain letters she wrote, probably hoping to have them smuggled out to northern newspapers to call attention to her imprisonment.

A young woman promenaded our streets yesterday, who, though by no means fair to look upon never moves abroad without attracting a crowd. We allude to Mary E. Walker, the Yankee Assistant Surgeon, who was caught within our lines last Spring, near Dalton. At her request she was, on yesterday, allowed to visit Gen. Gardner's headquarters, to consult him on the possibility of her obtaining a parole and being allowed to go North. The General promised to consider her case. This deluded female would have been sent North long ago but for the fact that since she has been incarcerated, she has been detected in some illicit correspondence.

General Gardner, a Georgian whose leg had been shattered at First Manassas, crippling him for life, interviewed her and came away with a positive impression, decidedly at odds with the ridiculing Richmond papers. He created a clever phrase for her appearance when he wrote of Mary as "the most personable and gentlemanly looking young woman I ever saw" and said she gave evidence of "good birth and refinement as well as superior intellect." In looking her over, Gardner felt compelled to lecture the gentlemanly young woman on the desirability of "feminine garb" and the futility of females serving in war. At this, more likely the general's kindly manner, she broke down and wept although she later explained that the weeping was due to the prospect of being released from imprisonment. She said that she returned Gardner's admonitions, telling him that men had no business dictating to women on their garb and that women "consumed half their energies by carrying about a bundle of clothes . . ."

Considering her declining health, and, no doubt, to get rid of a woman whose press notoriety was getting on his nerves, on August 12, 1864, Gardner ordered Mary's release.

Louisville

1

Together with several other prisoners, Mary was placed on the flag-of-truce steamer *New York* for the short passage down the James River to Fortress Monroe at Hampton Roads, inside Union lines. She took life-long pride in being exchanged "man for man" for a tall Confederate major.

After four months' imprisonment she was haggard, worn out, a wraith of skin and bones, having lost precious weight from her already small physique, and experiencing a recurring eye infection.

She recovered at home in Oswego and at her rented rooms in Washington, but only briefly before returning to the lecture circuit. She spoke on her war experiences and stumped for Abraham Lincoln in his campaign for reelection against Horatio Seymour, the Democratic governor of Mary's home state. (She did not hold a grudge against the president for his denial of her request to be officially assigned to a Washington hospital the previous January.)

The *Oswego Times,* on September 15, 1864, reported one speech she made that culminated in an appeal:

> I do believe that if the worst Copperhead could but see the President after a "Cabinet Meeting," just one glance at his careworn face, and feel that his great heart was constantly throbbing for the best interests of the most envied country in the World, they would forgive everything they censure him for, and put their shoulders to the wheel of the mammoth Republican car, instead of blocking the same.

She was in Oswego on election day in November 1864, casting her vote for Lincoln, and at that point felt strong enough to seek new war employment. Her medical work among the southern civilian populace inspired a letter to Major General W. T. Sherman, who commanded the Union's western armies, asking "most respectfully" that "a Commission be given me, with the rank of Majr, & that I be assigned to duty as surgeon of the female prisoners & the female refugees at Louisville, Ky." She said that "if there should be a hesitancy, on the ground that no woman has ever received such a commission," that "there has not been woman who has served Government in such a variety of ways of importance to the Great Cause which has elicited patriotism, that knows no sex."

She spoke of the Louisville position as a "military necessity," and told Sherman that there were between twenty-four and thirty female prisoners there and more than two hundred refugees, female and children, in the city.

After writing to Sherman, Mary discovered that the general was busy that September occupying Atlanta and preparing for his "march to the sea" with 68,000 men, but she also had an important visit with Assistant Adjutant General Edward Davis Townsend, soon to emerge as an important figure in her postwar life. To this officer she presented her papers and story of her services with emphasis on her work as "acting assistant surgeon" and unofficial spy while serving with the Fifty-second Ohio Regiment. Both roles, she pointed out, had been sanctioned by General George H. Thomas.

She had spent her own money throughout the war and now wanted to be paid.

Townsend telegraphed Thomas: "Is there anything due the woman and if so what amount for secret service or other services?" Mary's favorite general substantiated her work while associated with the Ohio regiment and "heartily recommended" that she be awarded the rank of major as "Her services have no doubt been valuable to the government & her efforts had been earnest and untiring . . ." He supplied Townsend the information that Dr. Walker had been a contract surgeon beginning on March 11, 1864, and suggested she be paid the standard eighty dollars a month for her services.

While she was not to receive the rank of major, nor any acknowledgment of a "commission" while with the Fifty-second, in early October Mary received the sum of $432.36 for her services with the army from March through August 1864. The adjutant general's office also granted part of the request she had made to General Sherman in September. While not granted a commission, she remained a civilian contract surgeon with the new assignment, a new salary of something over one hundred dollars a month, and a new title: "Surgeon in Charge" at the Louisville Female Military Prison hospital.

2

The Louisville prison, which had opened in early 1862, was not a permanent facility; it served as a collection, detention, and distribution center consisting of the prison proper, for male prisoners, on Broadway between Tenth and Eleventh Streets, and a facility for female civilian inmates on Twelfth Street. Except for severely ill or wounded inmates in the two-wing prison hospital (designated the Eruptive General Hospital—for contagious diseases—and Military Hospital No. 2), inmates were normally detained in Louisville only briefly before being transported to Union prisons in the north.

Mary reported for duty in late September 1864, and instantly discovered there would be neither prestige nor fulfillment in the title "Surgeon in Charge." The female facility, which housed mostly Confederate spies and others suspected of anti-Unionist enterprises and was regarded by its commandant as "no better than a brothel," did not welcome her. The all-male staff regarded her as a weirdly dressed interloper and Mary's impatience and overall authoritarian style did not serve her well.

She began her work, after inspecting the female wards, by insisting on better diets for the prisoners—coffee, soups, fresh beef, vegetables. She demanded cleanliness; replaced male cooks with females to improve the menu; tolerated "no Rebel songs or disloyal talk," no profanity, and no "familiarity" between inmates, guards, and other prison personnel. In a letter she wrote on January 5, 1865, to the commandant of the prison, she outlined these measures, adding that she would "not allow prisoners to abuse each other" or "to neglect their small children." In addition, she said, "I watched their rebel friends when they came here and would not allow them to pass letters without examining them, and would not allow talk I did not hear."

She brooked no insubordination between the prisoners and guards and wrote candidly of ordering one woman handcuffed for two hours for calling a guard a "D.S.B." to his face, and locking up others in a storehouse for "yelling out for Jeff Davis when rebel prisoners were passing."

In her "Incidents Connected with the Army," Mary recorded the "friendliness" between Union and Confederate soldiers, "plainly expressed by the vedettes on both sides, who occasionally called out to each other, one side asking for newspapers, the other side for tobacco." She wrote of Christmastime at the Louisville prison, when she wanted to give the Union troops there a gift and made a little Union flag for each of them. "Their weak voices seem clear in my ears at this time as they took the flags and said, 'I always did love the stars and stripes.'"

She wrote letters on behalf of certain prisoners, especially teenage girls, urging that they be freed and sent home; she treated their illnesses, improved their diets and sanitation, and earned the praise of her orderlies and of the prison's medical director, Dr. Edward Phelps. In August 1865, he wrote a glowing report on Mary's "active, energetic, and persevering spirit which had characterized her in her whole military career."

But to others, principally certain older female inmates, she was a Yankee ogre, condemned more for her dress than for her work among them. One of the prisoners wrote that her "dress was that of a man, but the braided hair and skinny, shrewish features were that of a woman. . . . a fiend in human guise." These women were accustomed to the lax methods of Dr. E. O. Brown, who had been the chief physician for the entire prison before Mary's arrival.

The females did not like the idea of another female giving orders and prescribing medicines—things women just did not do—and drew up a petition for her removal. Mary had no patience with such hard cases, female or not, and wrote to the commandant: "Give them their filth, unrestrained disloyalty and immorality and it will be satisfactory times with them. I am an eyesore to them. . . ."

Of the professional staff at the prison, Dr. Brown became a particular foe. Now in charge of only the male prisoners, he seems to have been rankled by Mary's presence from the start, probably considering her medical credentials bogus and her take-charge attitude insufferable. He insisted on visiting her wards and prescribing for her patients, forcing Mary to write to her superiors that Brown "has prejudiced or attempted to do so" her patients, and that he "told them that they were not to obey any of the orders . . . but those given by himself."

Brown, in turn, wrote to Dr. Robert C. Wood, the assistant surgeon general in Washington, "I regard Dr. M. E. Walker as incompetent to prescribe for the sick in the Female Prison, and would further state that her tyrannical conduct has been intolerable not only to the inmates of the Prison, but to myself."

He insisted she be examined by a military medical board, and at some unspecified date, she again faced a hostile panel of traditional male medicos. The chief examiner, a Dr. Gross, wrote to the surgeon general that Dr. Mary Walker was "utterly unqualified for her position" and that during her examination "she displayed ignorance of all branches of medicine."

Regardless of this criticism, the commandant of the Louisville Military Prison, Lieutenant Colonel J. H. Hammond, the man who admitted that the women's prison was "no better than a brothel," implored his superiors to let Mary have exclusive charge of her building and its inmates, and to keep Dr. Brown from further interference.

However, even with the enthusiastic support of Hammond and Dr. Edward Phelps, Mary had her fill of the otherwise thankless work in Louisville and in March 1865, after six months at the prison, requested a transfer. She wrote to Phelps that "it has been an untold task to keep this institution in a good condition morally & I am weary of the task & would much prefer to be where my services can be appreciated & I can do more good directly for the Cause."

Phelps remained true to her and granted her request, writing of her "superior talents and acquirements" which, he said in a key line, "enabled her to render even more service to her country than many of our efficient officers bearing full commissions."

3

Mary Walker's final assignment, which extended two months after the war's end, took her to an orphan and refugee asylum in Clarksville, Tennessee, on the Cumberland and Red

Rivers. Her duties there are virtually unknown, her activities an almost blank page in her record of service. It appears she reported for duty soon after the war's end, on April 9, 1865, and it is known that she created a small furor when she attended the local Episcopal church in an outfit that galled the vanquished southern populace. The *Louisville Journal* said, "She wore the Federal uniform, modified only by a short tunic above the knee, and cavalry boots, with shoulder straps showing her rank as a Major."

On another occasion she furthered her notoriety by adding a brace of pistols to her getup, and insensitively carried into the church a small American flag and bouquet tied with crepe which she nonchalantly placed on the chancel rail.

Her work in Clarksville, whatever it was, appears to have been brief. She was relieved of duty by an old nemesis, Dr. George E. Cooper of the Army of the Cumberland. This was the officer who, she said, had treated her with disdain from the moment she met him in Chattanooga early in 1864, just before her assignment to the Fifty-second Ohio Regiment.

She resigned from the army in June 1865, and received $766.16 for her work at the Louisville prison and Clarksville asylum.

4

Following her return to Washington, Mary began pushing her way through the tangled postwar bureaucracy. She continued to aspire for a commission as an army surgeon, setting her sights on a position as medical inspector in the Bureau of Refugees and Freedmen. After visiting the various bureaus in the War Department, she wrote directly to President Andrew

Johnson, describing her wartime services and asking for an assignment as a medical inspector with an officer's commission. She requested that the commission be awarded retroactive to the date of her appointment at the Louisville female prison.

The president knew of Mary Walker's name and some of her history of service to the Union and consulted Secretary of War Stanton in the matter, admitting that Dr. Walker "has performed service deserving the recognition of the Govt.— which I desire to give—if there is any way in which, or precedent, by which this may be done."

Stanton referred the case to the new surgeon general, M. B. Ames, who examined Mary's papers and reminded the president of her failed appearance before Dr. George Cooper's medical examining board prior to her attachment to the Fifty-second Ohio. Ames advised against a commission. This opinion was then referred to the judge advocate general, Joseph Holt, whose word carried heavy influence. He had been Stanton's predecessor as secretary of war, and presided over the trial of Lincoln's assassination conspirators in May and June 1865. While Judge Holt upheld the opinion that Mary be denied a commission, he recommended to the president that she be awarded some "commendatory acknowledgment" for her services.

On November 11, 1865, President Johnson signed a bill to award Dr. Mary Edwards Walker the Medal of Honor "for Meritorious Service."

The Medal

1

Before the Civil War, the United States awarded no military medals for valor in wartime. General George Washington introduced the "Badge of Military Merit" for "singularly meritorious action" but only three of them were awarded and it was discontinued after the Revolutionary War. In the 1846–1848 war with Mexico, a "Certificate of Merit"—a document and a two-dollar-a-month stipend—was occasionally bestowed on enlisted men for courageous acts, while officers were rewarded by a "brevet" increase in rank, a promotion without an increase in pay.

The award that became known as the Medal of Honor*

---

* Because it is customarily bestowed by the president "in the name of Congress," it is often, but erroneously, called the "Congressional Medal of Honor."

was first proposed by Gideon Welles, Lincoln's navy secretary, for enlisted personnel and petty officers to inspire them and "promote the efficiency of the Navy." The medal was envisioned as an American counterpart to England's Victoria Cross and Germany's Iron Cross. Senator James W. Grimes of Iowa, chairman of the Senate Naval Committee, sponsored the bill which passed both houses of Congress. Lincoln signed the legislation on December 21, 1861.

At about the time the naval medal was conceived, Lieutenant Colonel Edward Davis Townsend, assistant to Adjutant General Lorenzo Thomas in Washington, felt the army needed a medal for gallantry and drew up a letter to that effect. (Townsend was the friendly officer who assisted Mary Walker after her release from the Castle Thunder prison). The idea was forwarded to the general-in-chief, Winfield Scott, who rejected it. At age seventy-five, with fifty-five years in the army, Scott strongly opposed the European custom of awarding medals. (England had been doing so since 1816 with its Waterloo Medal and had inaugurated the Victoria Cross after the Crimean War of 1856 to 1858.)

Despite Scott's objection, the resolution creating the army's Medal of Honor was introduced by Senator Henry Wilson of Massachusetts, and signed by President Lincoln on July 12, 1862.

The army's medal was to be awarded, "to such non-commissioned officers and privates [officers became eligible in March 1863] as shall distinguish themselves by their gallantry in action, and other soldier-like qualities during the present insurrection."

Specific acts of bravery in the face of the enemy were not required since the original intent of the medal was to improve the morale and efficiency of the army, and no criteria was supplied to identify "soldier-like qualities."

The medal design was an inverted five-point star depicting Minerva, the goddess who represents both war and ancient Athenian wisdom, defending herself with a shield of stars and stripes, and an axe in a fasces (a bundle of bound sticks, a Roman symbol of authority) while her opponent, Discord, is armed with writhing serpents.

A total of 1,517 Medals of Honor were awarded during the Civil War, many of them passed out haphazardly. The worst example of the least-deserving recipients were the 309 medals awarded to members of the Twenty-seventh Maine, a regiment of nine-month volunteers, none of whom had been in battle. The men were to be discharged on June 30, 1863, as Lee's army invaded Pennsylvania, but were given the medal five days before Gettysburg as an incentive to stay at their post guarding Washington.

2

Mary Walker's appeal to President Andrew Johnson for a postwar commission and an assignment as medical inspector in the Bureau of Refugees and Freedmen seems, inadvertently, to have produced the recommendation that she be awarded the Medal of Honor. After he received her "case" from War Secretary Stanton, Judge Advocate General Joseph Holt of the War Department's Bureau of Military Justice submitted a twelve-page report on the issue. He concluded that Mary's imprisonment, exposure to danger and hardships, and her service to the sick and wounded made her "almost isolated in the history of the rebellion" and said to "signalize and perpetuate this fact," with the Medal of Honor "would seem to be desirable."

The president and Secretary Stanton agreed with Judge Holt's assessment and on January 24, 1866, Johnson authorized Colonel Edward D. Townsend to present Mary Walker with the medal.

The somewhat lackluster citation accompanying the medal was published in the *National Republican* together with an article expounding on her service. "This order is handsomely inscribed upon parchment and is the only compensation under the law that the President is empowered to bestow upon the doctor because she happens to be a woman," the newspaper reported. "Much of the service rendered by her to the Government could not have been accomplished by a man. She risked her life many times and nearly sacrificed her health in her efforts of patriotism, as time will hereafter tell. Until Congress can do Miss Walker some degree of pecuniary justice she must be content with the noble parchment testimonial of the President so justly bestowed. . . ."

The medal became Mary's proudest possession, and she wore it from the day it was presented until her death fifty-four years later. (In 1907, when she was given a new version of the medal, she wore them both.) The *Dictionary of American Biography* entry on Mary Edwards Walker states, "Her genuinely fine and kindly soul took great pride in the bronze medal given her by Congress for her war service."

3

In the summer of 1866, Mary received an invitation to serve as a delegate to a social science conference in Manchester, England. This was a fine opportunity for her to speak on her war experiences and on women's rights issues in general—certainly fitting subject matter for social scientists to hear—and she welcomed the chance for international exposure to her ideas.

She reached Liverpool in September, toured Scotland, and appeared at the Manchester gathering on October 8, her opening address on the question of women's suffrage. The October 12 *Glasgow Herald* described her as "a very slight figure . . . habited in a black surtout, fitting neatly to the body . . . The skirt of the surtout, in which is a side pocket from which a white handkerchief peeps, falls considerably below the knee." Her hair, "in regard to which the lady graduate has not denuded herself of the 'ornament of woman,'" the reporter wrote, "is tied close up behind, and is in proper feminine division from crown to forehead. A very little black straw hat completes her attire."

While fascinated by her clothing, the reporter did not forget the human being lying beneath them: "Her features are thin and small, and she is yet young, although showing a few of those lines which years always deepen. She is not pretty—not at least to admirers of plump and rosy faces—but in her manner she is engaging. . . . She will not break many hearts, but she may turn some heads."

The story of her medical degree, her Civil War service, her strange dress code, and outspoken views on women's issues, preceded her, and the British press made her somewhat of a celebrity. The December 1 *London Anglo-American Times* published President Andrew Johnson's citation for her Medal of Honor and wrote of her as the only female recipient of the distinguished medal and of her "strange adventures, thrilling experiences, important services and marvelous achievements" which "exceed anything that modern romance or fiction has produced." The paper went so far as to describe her as "one of the greatest benefactors of her sex and of the human race."

Paid speaking engagements enabled her to stay in Europe for a year, and while the press generally treated her respectfully, some of her audiences, and some medical publications, did not.

The *London Morning Star* reported on February 22, 1867, that the day before at St. James Hall, when she spoke of her prison experiences in Richmond (probably interspersed with an account of the medical services she performed there), she received catcalls from the medical students in the audience that required the police to clear them out. Elsewhere her dress theories were berated as ignorant, vapid, thin, "with no intellectual grasp or foundation." One British publication named her "the American Medical Nondescript" and another said her lecture "strengthens the opinion of those who hold that women had better not meddle in physic."

In Paris she toured the wards of the Hôtel Dieu and the London *Lancet* correspondent wrote on August 3, 1867:

> The peculiar costume of the lady added, of course, to the effect of the scene, and excited fresh curiosity. But

the doctoress was in no way daunted and walked com-
posedly through the wards, rather pleased than otherwise. She wore on her breast the medal received from
Congress and it is said . . . that she took some care to
show it off to advantage. . . . The doctoress, who is a
zealous tee-totaler, would drink nothing but water; still
there was drinking of healths, and a fraternal knocking
of glasses.

4

She returned to the United States later in August and
managed to continue touring, speaking to small-town book-
ings on her war experiences, suffrage, and equality for women,
mostly with mixed results to sparse audiences arranged by
various women's groups. She traveled through New York and
New England, Ohio, Kansas, and Missouri.

In Kansas City she was again arrested for her male clothing. The charges were quickly dismissed—a circumstance
parodied in doggerel in the *Kansas City Evening Star* on
December 11, 1869:

> *Policeman, spare those pants,*
> *And don't make any row;*
> *In youth, they sheltered me,*
> *And I'll protect them now.*

Mary proceeded into the Deep South with such stopovers
as Vicksburg and Jackson, Mississippi; New Orleans; and
Austin, Texas. Eventually her speaking engagements, which

had been minor to begin with, dried up, and she signed with a lyceum agent who booked her into dime museums and similar lowbrow venues where she talked about her war experiences while displaying her medal on her cutaway coat.

She returned, flat broke, to Washington after a ten-month tour and immersed herself in oratory on home rule for the capital city, and on women's issues, for the Mutual Dress Reform and Equal Rights Association, the Sons of Temperance, and the Central Woman's Suffrage Bureau.

MARY WALKER'S MEDAL OF HONOR CITATION

Rank and organization: Contract Acting Surgeon (civilian), U.S. Army. Places and dates: Battle of Bull Run, July 21, 1861; Patent Office Hospital, Washington, D.C., October 1861; Chattanooga, Tenn., following the Battle of Chickamauga, September 1863; Prisoner of War, April 10, 1864–August 12, 1864, Richmond, Va.; Battle of Atlanta, September 1864. Born 26 November 1832, Oswego, N.Y.

Whereas, It appears from official reports that Dr. Mary E. Walker, a graduate of medicine, has rendered valuable service to the Government, and her efforts have been earnest and untiring in a variety of ways, and that she was assigned to duty and served as an Assistant-Surgeon in charge of female prisoners at Louisville, Kentucky, upon the recommendation of Major-Generals Sherman and Thomas, and faithfully served as Contract Surgeon in the service of the United States, and has devoted herself with patriotic zeal to the sick and wounded soldiers, both in the field and hospital, to the detriment of her own health, and has also endured hardships as a prisoner-of-war four months in a Southern prison, while acting as a Contract-Surgeon; and,

Whereas, By reason of her not being a commissioned officer in the military service, a brevet or honorary rank cannot, under existing laws, be conferred upon her, and,

Whereas, In the opinion of the President an honorable recognition of her services and sufferings should be made, It is ordered that a testimonial thereof shall be hereby made and given to the said

Mary E. Walker, and the usual Medal of Honor for meritorious service shall be given her.

Given under my hand, in the City of Washington, D.C. this eleventh day of November, A.D. 1865. Andrew Johnson, President

Postwar

1

Although Mary Walker had performed countless nursing duties during her service, while always insisting on being recognized as a medical-school-graduate physician, among her first postwar campaigns was to speak on behalf of nurses who had served in hospitals behind the lines and in battlefield units. In the 1860s, nursing was not yet a recognized profession and had no real course of study; its practitioners learned the work as on-the-job volunteers. However, while loudly resisting being identified as a nurse, Mary stood with them, telling audiences of their war-caused distresses, their pitiful twenty-dollars-a-month pensions, and the public's general lack of gratitude for their service to the army.

In the early postwar years, she continued to write for *Sibyl*, the women's magazine published in Middletown, New York, contributing columns on such subjects as "The Woman's Mind"—on the superiority of the female reasoning process—and employment opportunities that women should be granted in wartime. On the latter subject she wrote, "I confess myself unable to see how respectable men can allow a laundress to go with their regiment, and shake their wise heads at the respectability of an educated lady acting as surgeon."

The issue that had practically defined her life continued to preoccupy her writing and oratory. She wrote and spoke on the folly of women wearing hoopskirts (which she said were "invented by the prostitutes of Paris") and crinolines, and on the obvious practicality of male dress. She continued to remain active in the National Dress Reform Association, later the Mutual Dress Reform and Equal Rights Association, which met for a convention in Syracuse in June 1866, and elected her as its president.

That summer's convention proved to be a spectacular success, thanks to the press notoriety that Mary received after she had another run-in with the law. The story was covered in detail in the June 14, 1866, issue of the *New York Evening Express,* and also in the *New York Sun* and *The New York Times.*

The story told of Mary, who was browsing in a Manhattan millinery shop, was that she caught the attention of some of the other women shoppers and their children with her "male costume." Some anxious conversation ensued among the disturbed ladies, and the shop owner reacted by asking the police to escort Mary from the premises. Naturally, she resisted. When asked her address she said, "Anywhere the Stars and Stripes fly," and insisted on being taken to the precinct headquarters. She and a policeman were followed by a group of idlers with nothing better to do.

At the station, Mary refused to utter her name but did permit the desk sergeant to read it on the reverse side of her Medal of Honor, which she wore on the lapel of her male-styled suit coat. Then, when the sergeant offered to have an officer usher her through the crowd, she said, "When I wish the protection of a policeman I will ask an intelligent one."

Before she left the station she filed charges of improper conduct against the patrolman who had escorted her there, and a few days later the case opened before the metropolitan police commissioner, Thomas Coxon Acton. A number of reporters covered the proceedings, delighting in the opportunity to describe the outfit that caused such commotion in the milliner's shop. Mary was depicted in the *New York Tribune* as,

Brevet Major of the United States Volunteers . . . an attractive woman who may have seen thirty summers [who] was habited in black broadcloth, her coat, from the shoulders to the waist, closely resembling a woman's ordinary attire; but from the waist downward the cut of both coat and pantaloons is masculine. Her hat is the merest chip of straw. . . . Her dainty parasol, her bijoutry [jewelry], indeed everything but the ample pantaloons and coat terminating at the knees betokened the moderately fashionable woman.

(Being described as "attractive," at least, cancelled the Richmond papers' insistence that she was ugly.)

Another newspaper report wrote sympathetically of her "suit of fine black broadcloth" that "consisted of a dress or gown gathered at the waist in the manner of ordinary dresses, and a skirt reaching thence a little below the knee." Underneath, the reporter said, were pantaloons of the same material, "loosely fitting the limbs, and open at the feet as in male attire." The ensemble "was very suggestive of convenience, ease of motion and personal neatness. The wearer had the air of a lady with perhaps a slight tinge of (feminine) smartness and loquacity."

Her "loquacity"—the Richmond press used the word "chatty"—clearly referred to Mary's spirited defense of her mode of dress, and dress reform in general. She explained to the court that she was "a practicing physician and surgeon," and how she had worn her outfit in the city many times previously and been treated courteously. She said she did not care to wipe up dirt and miscellaneous filth with a long dress, nor wear hoops that blew skyward in the wind, exposing her limbs.

The police officer's lawyer stated that wearing male clothing was clearly an offense that caused "public excitement" and that under the law it was a misdemeanor, punishable by fine or, if repeated, incarceration.

Commissioner Acton, at the end of the proceeding, told Mary, "I consider, madame, that you have as good a right to wear that clothing as I have to wear mine and he [the patrolman] has no more right to arrest you for it than he has of me. But if you were creating a disturbance, and there was a mob gathered there, he would be justified in removing you. He was fearful that you would be insulted."

At the end of his summation he announced, probably playing to the newspapermen gathered in the room, "You are smarter than most ladies in the City of New York. I would have no hesitation in letting you go your own way . . . but he [the patrolman] thought you a weak woman, needing protection." Then, turning to the officer, Acton said, "Let her go, she can take care of herself. Never arrest her again." To which, one reporter wrote, "there was loud laughter."

Mary's arrest and "trial" provided a publicity boost for the June dress-reform convention in Syracuse, but she topped the story in her inaugural speech as president when she proposed a wicked punishment for the former Confederate president, Jefferson Davis. She said he should be condemned to be treated like a woman, forced to wear a corset and hoopskirts, and do housework in a four-story home. She said this would be a worse sentence than any prison term.

The press was also captivated by a demonstration Mary staged at the convention hall. The *New York World* reported on June 14 on the particular outfit she had invented, and the women she introduced to model it: "a big woman, an elderly woman, a young girl, and herself as a 'slight figure.'"

The conference ended with the reformers adopting resolutions to thank Commissioner Acton "for his decision in Dr. Walker's case in regard to the rights of women to walk the streets of New York clothed in a physiological manner," and New York editors and reporters for "defending" Dr. Walker "to dress in a manner that comports with freedom of motion, health and morality."

2

Mary's postwar work included writing two books, one titled, for reasons unknown, *Hit* (1871), which was partly autobiographical, mostly philosophical, with chapters on love, marriage, divorce, dress reform, women's suffrage, and religion. Another, *Unmasked, or the Science of Immorality, To Gentlemen by a Woman Physician and Surgeon* (1878), gave unprecedentedly candid views on such sensational and taboo subjects for the era as hermaphrodites, morning sickness, the hymen, barrenness, and kissing and social diseases (the last two of which she believed were linked).

She set up a medical practice in Washington, D.C., and from the end of the war through the 1870s worked with the band of suffragettes headquartered in the capitol that included some of the luminaries of the Seneca Falls Convention of 1848. With Susan B. Anthony, Lucy Stone, Mary Livermore, and attorney Belva Lockwood, with whom she shared a flat, she buttonholed congressmen, collected petitions, and staged demonstrations out of the group's Central Women's Suffrage Bureau.

In 1871 she helped organize a march in Washington that included prominent suffragettes and the former slave and eminent abolitionist, Frederick Douglass. The march was directed to registration places where the women demanded to be allowed to vote. Once, when they were turned away, Mary said to one of officials, "Gentlemen, these women have assembled to exercise the right of citizens of a professed-to-be republican country, and if you debar them of the right to register, you but add new proof that this is a tyrannical government, sustained by force and not by justice."

In 1881 she announced her own candidacy for the United States Senate, proclaiming she was the ideal candidate since her brain was unsullied by drugs, liquor, or tobacco. These strong attributes did not win over the party bosses, however, and she was not nominated by New York Democrats.

Among the suffragettes, Mary was most often the butt of rude jokes, egg bombardment by unruly boys, and the disapproval by both sexes. She was arrested several times for "masquerading in men's clothing," welcoming the misdemeanor charges and the publicity that followed.

Her sister revolutionaries did not agree with her ways and eventually began regarding her as an embarrassment to the women's rights cause. Lockwood and her cohorts, some of whom had dallied with Amelia Bloomer's pantaloon experiment but had deserted it for conventional women's dress (as did Bloomer herself), went so far as to suggest to Mary that she follow their example.

The idea enraged her and she refused to consider it, continuing to dress in her black broadcloth suit, often with a matching dress over the trousers. She also designed a pantsuit which, she said, would "improve female health and discourage seduction": a linen "undersuit" with a high neck, loose waist, long sleeves and wristbands, and "whole drawers" folded over the ankles with the stockings adjusted over them. This ensemble resulted in "keeping the ankles warm and also keeping the stockings arranged without elastic or other bands or any troublesome or injurious arrangement, most of which impeded the circulation and produce varicose veins, and weariness in walking." Over the undersuit were trousers "made like men's, either buttoned to the waist of the undershirt or arranged with the usual suspenders." She described the dress as hanging free of the body, "the waist and skirt of one piece like a sack coat and falling to the knees, thus preventing it being stepped upon while descending stairs, or of becoming soiled in rainy days—but principally because of a needed relief to women from its shortness."

As the years passed Mary's choice of clothing grew more bizarre and masculine, and by the 1880s she routinely wore a high-collared shirt, tie, frock coat, and striped trousers; when on the lecture platform or at social gatherings she favored a full evening dress, with swallowtail coat, cravat, and occasionally a cape plus a silk topper and walking stick. For her single nod to femininity she wore her hair in curls so that, she said, "everybody would know that I was a woman."

(Humorist Edward W. "Bill" Nye of the New York *World* described her as "a self-made man.")

Her outfit included one unique touch of her own design. She is credited with inventing the inside neck band on men's shirts, which protects the skin from chafing from the collar button.

Eventually she became something of a pariah among the women's rights activists. Her aggressiveness and growing eccentricities, and her coupling the right-to-vote campaign with her dress reform mania, embarrassed the stalwarts.

Still, she persisted, stubbornly demanding to be heard, and eventually broke with Susan B. Anthony, Lucy Stone, and other pioneers of the women's vote. Mary's split with the women with whom she once shared stages and podiums was not exclusively a dispute over her manner of dress. The activists of the suffrage movement had long since agreed that the only realistic path to the vote was through a Constitutional amendment. With what some of her contemporaries thought was willful contrariness, Mary made it clear that she had no faith in this approach. She believed in civil disobedience and such measures as mass demonstrations at registration and voting places as the key to enforcing "the mechanism for suffrage" already present in the Constitution. Since that sacred document declared every state to have a republican form of government, denying the vote to women reduced the states to what she called "half-republics."

Mary presented her "Crowning Constitutional Argument" in a pamphlet in 1907, and as late as 1916, at age 83, made an address before the New York State Judiciary Committee in favor of a bill to end voting discrimination against women.

Her remarks were significant in that she had lashed out at suffrage leaders Elizabeth Cady Stanton and Susan B. Anthony—both then deceased—for their "determined effort . . . with the most disreputable trickery" in undermining her efforts to explain her "Crowning Constitutional Argument." Her memory unaffected by her years, she recalled an 1873 women's rights meeting at Lincoln Hall in Washington, D.C., in which "Mrs. Stanton" only yielded the platform to her when she forced the matter and won the audience's approval. She spoke of a meeting in Albany on March 9, 1910, in which two activist women, one representing Elizabeth Stanton (who had died in 1902), begged Mary "not to speak, as it would spoil everything"—meaning the work toward a Constitutional amendment.

Mary denied that the failure to get across an understanding of her "Argument" was due to her mode of dress. "I here and now make it plain that *dress* has nothing to do with the matter; but some women are made to believe that it does have . . ."

Despite her spirited address, the 1916 New York bill to end voter discrimination died. Three years later, in the year of Mary's death, the efforts of the suffrage movement at last paid the great dividend with passage of the Nineteenth Amendment to the Constitution, granting the vote to women.

Hard Times

1

Since it was impossible for Mary Walker to earn a comfortable living as a physician, or as a writer or lecturer, she became relentless in seeking to supplement her income through relief from the government, both for a pension and for employment.

Late in 1871 she wrote to her old acquaintance, Edward D. Townsend, now the army's adjutant general, requesting that he send a letter to the commissioner of pensions stating that she had been a "contract surgeon" with the army during the Civil War. Townsend complied, amending the request to "assistant contract surgeon." In the meantime, she flooded the War Department and other government bureaus with paperwork—testimonial letters, orders and regulations, legal opinions, and affidavits, in support of her appeal for a pension, based upon a medical disability. She had developed eye problems, which she attributed to her imprisonment, and, in November 1876, after a ten-year campaign, she was awarded an $8.50-a-month pittance for "atrophy of the nerves of the eyes" deriving from her incarceration, from April through August 1864, at Castle Thunder in Richmond.

In May 1876, after five years of effort to increase her "pension," she persuaded a New York congressman to introduce a bill for her "relief," demanding a settlement of ten thousand dollars "for money expended and injury received in the late war." The bill died in committee.

Also in 1876, the commissioner of the pension office presented a revealing, if baffling, argument in turning down an appeal Mary had made directly to him. The commissioner not only acknowledged her role as a Union spy but indicated that her capture by the Confederates had been part of her orders. "Your appointment as such contract surgeon," he wrote, "was made for the purpose, not of performing of duties pertaining to such office, but that you might be captured by the enemy to enable you to obtain information concerning their military affairs; in other words, you were to act in the role of a spy for the United States military authorities." Then, with amazing illogic, he stated, "It was held . . . that at the time of your capture by the enemy, you were not actually performing the duties of an assistant surgeon or acting assistant surgeon with any military force in the field . . . therefore, your claim to pension on account of disease of eyes contracted while a prisoner of war does not come within the purview of the general pension law."

For another fourteen years Mary continued her paper barrage for "arrears in pay" and adjustment of her pension. Over twenty bills were introduced in Congress on her behalf, but not until 1890, during the Benjamin Harrison administration, did she have any success. In that year her pension was adjusted to twenty dollars a month "for her services in the Civil War," the sum *including* the $8.50 she had been receiving since 1876.

Her father died in 1880, and the farm which he willed to her was encumbered by a one-thousand-dollar mortgage. It also fell to her to care for her mother, now nearly eighty and in failing health. Mary needed to earn a dependable living, therefore her efforts in Washington turned to gaining federal employment. Again her appeals were directed up and down the chain of command, from presidents to congressmen to cabinet members and minor office holders.

Finally, in 1881, after the assassination of James A. Garfield promoted New Yorker Chester A. Arthur to the presidency, she wangled a post as clerk in the mail room of a department she knew well, the Pensions Office of the Department of the Interior. She held the job from April 1882 until June 1883, when she was fired. Her employment was marked, her superiors said, by her chronic absenteeism, abrasive nature, and "violent temper." One supervisor said she was "a firebrand in our midst. Insulting to the ladies and inattentive to her duties." He said she complained about everything, read newspapers, and neglected her work.

Mary was convinced there was a conspiracy to remove her because she attempted to correct certain abuses she found in the operation of the office. But when these claims were rejected and she was dismissed, she refused to accept the decision and filed voluminous paperwork in her defense. Her case reached the office of an assistant attorney general but he found no reason to reverse the firing.

To make ends meet, she signed on with the Chicago-based Kohl and Middleton Agency, which contracted with celebrities and produced stage lectures and exhibitions in "dime museums" around the country. The museums, forerunners of carnival sideshows, were a popular (and cheap) amusement outlet in the 1880s, an outgrowth of showman P. T. Barnum's American Museum in Lower Manhattan, which opened in 1841. For the dime ticket, museum patrons could gaze at attractions, living and dead, such as sword swallowers, Zulu warriors, "Circassian beauties," "Baby Alice, The Midget Wonder," shrunken heads, Peruvian mummies, two-headed pigs, and a variety of other "freaks of nature."

While the dime museums were best known for their "sensational entertainment," they also presented talks and stage performances by celebrities of the day. Kohl and Middleton was a respectable and prosperous booking agency with such clients as escape artist Harry Houdini and the Western character Martha "Calamity Jane" Canary. Mary did well in her association with them, earning $150 a month speaking on her dress ideas, suffrage, the evils of tobacco, and her war experiences. She toured Chicago, Toledo, Cincinnati, Buffalo, New York City, and Detroit in 1887 and 1888, and returned for engagements in 1893.

Some saw her dime museum performances as humiliating. During the 1893 tour, the *Toledo Blade* reported on March 25 on her appearance at a museum called Wonderland under the heading,

DR. MARY WALKER
FROM THE PLATFORM OF PRINCES
TO THE STAGE OF FREAKS

and said, "There was a time when this remarkable woman stood upon the same platform of Presidents and the world's greatest women. There is something grotesque in her appearance on the stage built for freaks."

2

She claimed to be a political independent, but in fact she was a staunch Democrat, and in 1890 even declared herself a Democratic candidate for Congress. While nothing came of this beyond her announcement, she was never hesitant to show her Democrat colors.

She was outspoken against Ulysses S. Grant in 1868 and 1872, indeed she despised the Union's great general, more for his whiskey drinking, cigar smoking, and tendency to appoint family members and cronies to government posts, than for his Republican politics.

One can only ponder, since there is no record of her reaction, what Mary had thought of a notable event in the second Grant administration, the first woman presidential candidate. Victoria Clafin Woodhull, age thirty-four, was nominated on May 10, 1872, at a convention in New York

City, by a group of about five hundred dissidents attending the National Woman Suffrage Association convention in the city. The delegates, calling themselves variously the People's Party, the Equal Rights Party, and the National Radical Reformers—the latter a name that may have attracted Mary's attention—represented twenty-six states and four territories. The breakaway party nominated Frederick Douglass, with whom Mary had marched in suffrage parades, as Woodhull's vice presidential running mate, but the ticket received only a few thousand popular votes.

Without doubt, Mary would have been outraged that Woodhull, a free-love advocate, one-time spiritualist, and editor of a scandal sheet, could be a candidate for anything other than a jail cell, where, in fact, Woodhull spent election day in 1872. She had been charged with obscenity, for printing the salacious details of a particularly juicy scandal involving the eminent Henry Ward Beecher, pastor of Brooklyn's Plymouth Church. Despite her differences with Mary Walker, Victoria Woodhull and her sister, Tennessee, were promoters in the late 1860s and early 1870s, of male-styled dress somewhat similar to the outfit Mary wore.

Mary had a low regard for the Republican Rutherford B. Hayes in spite of the fact that during his administration her lawyer friend Belva Lockwood became the first woman admitted to practice before the United States Supreme Court. Mary would not have supported James A. Garfield in 1880, although she must have been delighted that the American Red Cross was organized during his brief preassassination tenure. Nor would she have cast a vote for the Republican successor to Garfield, Chester A. Arthur, even though it was during the Arthur presidency that she found federal employment in Washington.

She stood in favor of Grover Cleveland's two bids for the presidency, in 1885 and 1893. In both these presidential campaigns, Cleveland, among the other candidates, was opposed by Belva Lockwood, representing the National Equal Rights Party. But Mary may have been smarting at the rejection of her perennial dress-reform campaign and for being regarded as too eccentric and controversial by Lockwood and other prominent suffragettes.

Mary remained a faithful supporter of William Jennings Bryan in all three of his campaigns for the presidency—1896, 1900, and 1908.

In 1901 she joined the Kansas temperance agitator Carrie Nation and several militant suffragettes in vilifying the assassinated President William McKinley. In one of Mary's soapbox orations, she inexplicably and without explanation blamed the murder on his vice president, Theodore Roosevelt. She added to this mad statement that it was no worse for the assassin Leon Czolgosz to kill McKinley than for the state of New York to execute Czolgosz—a reasoning lost on most of her auditors. For these utterances a mob threatened her and she had to be rescued by local police.

(Years later her enmity toward Roosevelt cropped up again when, as she was introduced to young Franklin Delano Roosevelt, then secretary of the navy, she informed him of her low regard for his cousin "Teddy.")

In 1917, together with many other prominent suffragettes and women's rights fighters, Mary opposed America's entry into the war with Germany, and persisted in calling the

Democratic President "Kaiser Wilson." She argued, "Why should women support the war effort when we're not even allowed to vote for the government which declares that war?"

3

Mary retired to her Oswego farm in about 1891, but even in this rustic setting she was a magnet for controversy. Her tenant farmers sued her for various grievances as she grew increasingly eccentric, lonely, and poor. Some who knew her then said she alienated what few friends she had.

She talked of converting the farm into a "Home Sanitarium School for consumptives," and even issued a brochure to promote the idea, writing of the recuperative nature of the Oswego area, its "idyllic setting," free from city noise and polluting smoke.

Another of her dreams was described in *Metropolitan Magazine* in December 1895, in an article on her plans for a "new woman's colony," a training school for young women to learn homemaking and the ways of farm life. This idea represented a strange turnaround. Mary had devoted much of her life to preaching the need for women to leave hearth and home if they chose to do so, and challenge male dominance of the professions. Her own failure to support herself as a physician seems to have made her reflective of the life her beloved mother led.

A New York newspaper reported in 1897 her plans for an "Adamless Eden" on a tract of her farmland, a colony for young women to pledge themselves to remain unmarried and devote their time to work and study, presumably toward entering the professions. Another more sensation-minded newspaper, bent on ridiculing Oswego's noted eccentric, picked up the story and elaborated nonsensically that the colony would extend its all-female residents even to the farm's animals, and that roosters and turkey gobblers would be sought out and eliminated.

In November 1893, Mary was interviewed at her home by the *Nashua Telegraph*. The reporter was completely won over by her, discovering Dr. Walker to be quite at odds with her curmudgeon's reputation. He said she was "one of the most pleasant and courteous persons to interview that can be imagined and answered all of the reporter's questions in a most kindly manner." He wrote:

> She is called a crank, insane, and has been abused by the press and in private . . . and yet to sit down and talk with her on any subject relating to the welfare or uplifting of her fellowmen and women she at once appears as a liberal minded, earnest and self sacrificing advocate of all methods that tend to the ennobling or elevating of her fellow creatures. Many of her ideas in this respect are advanced and doubtless far ahead of the majority of people and yet they are for the betterment of society rather than for its debasement.

The writer described her as "now over fifty years of age [she was sixty-three], but still robust," and ended the article by observing, "There are many more pretentious places than this old-fashioned house, but there is no place where contentment and peace are more in evidence than in Dr. Mary Walker's Colony of One."

DR. MARY'S PRESCRIPTIONS

True conjugal companionship is the greatest blessing of which mortals can conceive in this life—to know that there is supreme interest in *one* individual, and that it is reciprocated.

There cannot be love without respect, and there cannot be respect unless there is implicit confidence.

Women cannot be deprived of God-given rights . . . without men being sufferers as well as women.

The first great principle in the clothing of the body is that there shall be perfect freedom of motion; the second, that there should be equal distribution of the clothing; the third, that the arrangement should be such that as little of vitality should be expended in carrying it about as is possible.

There is nothing in creation that is so loathed by those who do not use it as is Tobacco in its various preparations.

No one can be found who cannot see the great wrongs resulting from excessive drinking, for they are so defined that there is no mistaking them.

Deity intended a free and full development of all of woman's powers, as well as man's, and gave her a mind to decide for herself in all things.

Men do not respect women who do not respect their own individuality.

To be deprived of a Divorce is like being shut up in a prison because someone attempted to kill you.

No kind of Labor should be despised.

No Religion is true and genuine, it matters not what church its representatives belong to, unless it is something that makes homes happy and ennobles life generally.

The most charming of all things earthly is the thought of dying a beautiful death. . . .

Last Battle

1

She continued to commute between Oswego and Washington, D.C., until two years before her death. At home she became involved in disputes over the Bunker Hill property, quarreling with the neighbors who were actually farming the land until she drove them all off, some taking her to court for money owed to them. In Washington, she made the customary rounds, visiting legislators, old friends, and various federal officials, making occasional appearances at women's rights or suffrage conferences, talking to journalists, searching for somebody to listen to her plea for an increase in her pension.

In 1914 she decided to seek membership in the Daughters of the American Revolution and submitted her credentials as great-granddaughter of Revolutionary War soldier Jessie Snow of Hardwich, Massachusetts. The New York office of the DAR turned down her application on the specious basis that theirs was a woman's organization and Mary had repudiated womanhood by her mode of dress. In earlier times, Mary would have delighted in fighting this decision, visiting the DAR office in a froth, wearing the malest of her outfits, making demands, inviting the press. But her fighting days were past and she was content to be admitted to the St. Louis DAR chapter.

In 1917, when Mary was eighty-five, she suffered a fall on the Capitol steps, returned to her Oswego farm to recuperate, but never fully recovered. That year she faced another reversal, the worst in her tumultuous life: Fifty-two years after she was awarded the Medal of Honor, it was taken away.

The medal and the criteria for earning it had been under scrutiny for decades. In 1876, following the Custer battle in Montana Territory, some officers were recommending the medal for whole units who survived the disastrous campaign. Among others, General Alfred Terry, the veteran Indian fighter, spoke out against such wholesale awardings, saying, "Medals of Honor are not intended for ordinary good conduct, but for conspicuous acts of gallantry."

In 1890, a Medal of Honor Legion was organized to end the abuse caused by the original wording of the criteria, which made eligible for the award "such noncommissioned officers and privates as shall distinguish themselves by their gallantry in action, and other soldier-like qualities." In 1892, a new interpretation was presented by Adjutant General J. C. Kelton stating, "Medals of Honor should be awarded to officers or enlisted men for distinguished bravery in action, while Certificates of Merit should, under the law, be awarded for distinguished service, whether in action or otherwise. . . ."

Even stronger wording was added in 1897, when President McKinley directed the army to establish new medal policies. The revised regulations stipulated that the Medal of Honor was to be awarded for "gallantry and intrepidity" above and beyond the call of duty, and that a potential recipient had to be recommended by a disinterested party. This last requirement put an end to Civil War veterans "applying" for the medal themselves.

Theodore Roosevelt, who yearned for the medal and believed he had earned it, had been denied the decoration for his July 1, 1898, charge up San Juan Hill, Cuba,* yet he strengthened and elevated the award. He issued an executive order in 1905 calling for an "impressive ceremonial" in which the president, as commander-in-chief of American military forces, or his representative, would personally make the medal presentations.

The most radical event in the history of the award began in 1916, at a time when more than twenty-five hundred medals had been awarded, the vast majority of them for Civil War exploits. That year a bill passed in Congress for an army and navy Medal of Honor Roll listing those who had earned the decoration for "action involving actual conflict with the enemy, distinguished by conspicuous gallantry or intrepidity, at the risk of life, above and beyond the call of duty."

---

* On January 16, 2001, eighty-one years after his death, in a White House ceremony conducted by President Bill Clinton, Roosevelt was awarded the Medal of Honor for his exploits with his Rough Rider regiment in the Spanish-American War. He is the only president to have received the award.

Following this, a subsection of the National Defense Act of June 1916 was written in preparation for the possibility that the United States would enter the Grear War in Europe. The provision called for the secretary of war to appoint a board of retired army officers to investigate and determine if any Medals of Honor had been awarded for any cause other than "distinguished conduct in action involving actual conflict with an enemy."

In January 1917, a board of five retired generals submitted their report. The panel was led by the army's Lieutenant General Nelson A. Miles, a distinguished seventy-six-year-old Medal of Honor recipient with forty-two years service in Indian campaigns and the Civil War. He and the others examined 2,625 medal "cases" and reported that 911 of the awards did not meet the accepted criteria and were to be "stricken from the list."

Among the medals stricken, effective on February 15, 1917, were: the 555 given in 1863 to the twenty-seventh Maine Volunteer Infantry as an inducement for them to remain in service; the twenty-nine given to the officers and enlisted men who escorted the remains of President Lincoln to Springfield, Illinois, for interment following his assassination; the one presented to a lieutenant colonel who, in 1872, wrote the War Department requesting the medal for his Civil War services; the one given to William Frederick "Buffalo Bill" Cody, for his work as a civilian scout in Indian campaigns; and the medal awarded on November 11, 1865, to Mary Edwards Walker, civilian contract surgeon with the Union army.

In striking Mary Walker's medal the board stated that her service "does not appear to have been distinguished in action or otherwise," and called attention to the refusal by War Secretary Stanton to appoint her a full-fledged surgeon or grant her numerous appeals for a commission. The board also mentioned the "adverse report of the Surgeon General" of September 30, 1865. In this report, Dr. M. B. Ames, upon studying her request for a commission and elevation to surgeon, had reported to President Johnson of Mary's rejection by a medical examining board prior to her attachment to the Fifty-second Ohio Regiment.

Mary was infuriated at the news of the board's decision to annul her medal. She petitioned the generals who sat in judgment of her, sent them voluminous amounts of paper that attested to her noble and tireless work during the war, but her efforts were to no avail. The board would not rereview the matter, stating it found "no evidence of distinguished gallantry in her case."

Accustomed to rejection, she responded to the problem as she had done when the army refused her a commission. On that occasion she made herself to a uniform and promoted herself to a major. When the army struck her medal from the rolls she simply refused to acknowledge the decision. Nor did she surrender her medal—actually her medals, since she occasionally wore both the old and new designs—and the army wisely did not force the issue.

She continued to wear her medal until her death.

2

Mary Walker's Civil War service lasted close to three years, discounting the months she spent at home and at Hygeia College in New York after her work at the Indiana Hospital ended. In her long life she witnessed from afar two other wars, the six-week Spanish-American campaign and the stupendous bloodshed of World War I, and lived through the assassinations of three American presidents. She derived some satisfaction in seeing the fruition of some of her lifelong causes: the popular election of senators, the 1919 amendment on woman's suffrage, the coming of prohibition, the wearing of trousers by women who worked in war and munitions factories, and the advances of women in medicine. (In Civil War times there were fewer than two hundred female physicians in America; by the time she died there were perhaps fifty times that number.)

She remained intensely patriotic to the end of her life. Just before World War I she wrote a poem ending with:

When I am buried 'neath the ground,
Wrap that flag my corpse around,
Plant that flag above my grave,
There let it wave! Let it wave!

And, in 1917, with America on the brink of entering the war in Europe, she sent a cable to Kaiser Wilhelm of Germany calling on him to stop the war and inviting him to a peace conference at her farm at Bunker Hill. Her only rules were that she would permit no intoxicating drinks and no smoking.

In the last interview she gave, published in the *Syracuse Post-Standard* three days after her death, she said,

Presidents and cabinet ministers and great generals were glad to meet and listen to me. I was younger then, and I was working for our soldier boys, just as so many girls and young women are working in the Red Cross for our boys who are over there [actually, the war in Europe had ended three months earlier]. . . . Now I am alone with the infirmities of age fast weighing me down and practically penniless, and no one wants to be bothered with me. . . . But it is the same experiences that have come to others, and why should I complain?

Mary Edwards Walker died on February 21, 1919, at the age of eighty-six, at the home of friends in Oswego. She had no fear of death, writing in her 1871 book, *Hit: Essays on Women's Rights,* "The most charming of all things earthly is the thought of dying a beautiful death . . ."

She left instructions for a simple funeral and on February 24 was buried in her black "male habiliments" suit, with an American flag over her casket.

A good epitaph for her would have been the editorial remarks made in *The New York Times* on March 25, 1912: ". . . she had a sort of dignity, and about her an essential goodness . . ."

Or, the statement by Secretary of War Edwin M. Stanton: "She lived a life of determined unconventionality. . . ."

She lies in a family plot with her parents, Alvah and Vesta Whitcomb Walker, in the Oswego Rural-Union Cemetery about two miles from her home. On the grave today, surrounded by a white picket fence, is a family monument in the shape of an obelisk engraved with all the Walker names, and a Civil War veteran's plaque for Mary.

3

The Bunker Hill farmhouse was destroyed by fire in the 1940s and the property, in a wooded area, has been vacant ever since. A historical marker commemorates Dr. Mary Walker's presence there in times past, her service in the Civil War, and her award of the Medal of Honor.

All other honors and recognition she has received came long after her death.

A memorial at Arlington National Cemetery, dedicated to American women in military service, features her story with a photograph.

The Walker Army Reserve Center in Michigan, a training facility for personnel of the Army Reserve's 334th Medical Group, is named for her. When the center opened in 2001, the commanding officer said, "We name this center for her because she was a great citizen soldier. . . ."

In 1982, the U.S. Postal Service issued a twenty-cent stamp bearing her likeness to commemorate the 150th anniversary of her birth.

Her Medal of Honor, the single possession she prized above all others, she never relinquished in the fifty-four years after it was presented to her, even after it was stricken from the rolls in 1917. She lived two years and six days after that final, debilitating blow to the record of her Civil War service and to her pride.*

---

* Her Medal of Honor is part of the collection of the Oswego County, New York, Historical Society. The later, redesigned medal, issued many years after the first, was also part of the collection until it was stolen while on loan in 1986 to the Rome, New York, Historical Society. The second medal has not yet been recovered.

Epilogue

On June 10, 1977, President Jimmy Carter signed a bill reinstating Mary Edwards Walker's Medal of Honor.*

The restoration came as the result of years of indefatigable work by Mary Walker's grand-niece, Mrs. Helen Hay Wilson of Washington, D.C., who led the campaign to have the medal reinstated. Along with Ann Walker, also of Washington and identified in U.S. Postal Service news releases as a distant relative of Mary's family, Wilson mounted a lobbying campaign in the late 1960s to restore Mary's medal on the grounds that the 1917 revocation of the award had been the result of gender bias. This work began to have effect when, in November 1974, Ann Walker received an unusually candid

---

* In 1989, the army also restored Medals of Honor to five civilian scouts of the Indian campaigns, including the medal awarded to William Frederick "Buffalo Bill" Cody that had been stricken, along with Mary Walker's, in 1917.

letter from the Senate Veterans Affairs Committee stating, "It's clear your great-grand-aunt was not only courageous during the term she served as a contract doctor in the Union Army, but also as an outspoken proponent of feminine rights. Both as a doctor and feminist, she was much ahead of her time and, as is usual, she was not regarded kindly by many of her contemporaries. Today she appears prophetic."

The Army Board of Corrections of Military Records agreed, ruling that had it not been for her sex, Mary Walker would have been commissioned in 1861. It concluded that, "when consideration is given to her total contribution, her acts of distinguished gallantry, self-sacrifice, patriotism, dedication, and unflinching loyalty to her country, despite the apparent discrimination because of her sex, the award of the Medal of Honor appears to have been appropriate." In its disagreement with the 1917 ruling, the board stated that "there is ample evidence to show distinguished gallantry at the risk of life in the face of the enemy" and that the award "was in consonance with the criteria established by the Act of 17 April 1916 and in keeping with the highest traditions of the military service."

The officers of the board ordered "That all the Department of the Army records pertaining to Mary Edwards Walker be corrected to show that she was validly awarded the Medal of Honor by President [Andrew] Johnson in 1865; that her name was selected to be entered on the Medal of Honor Roll, in accordance with the Act of 3 June 1916, and that the action taken in 1917 to remove her name from the Medal of Honor Roll is void and of no force, or effect."

Not all agreed with the reinstatement. Some military officers asked if Mary Walker's service, while no doubt selfless and even valiant, warranted the same medal awarded to such distinguished heroes as Eddie Rickenbacker, Alvin York, Sam Woodfill, Douglas MacArthur, and Audie Murphy. Did she earn a medal so coveted that Harry Truman said he would trade the presidency for it, one that General George S. Patton said he would trade his soul for? Retired Army Colonel Wil Ebel, in an article in *The Retired Officer Magazine* in July 1977, spoke for many of his colleagues in writing, "In the author's view, the Army provided no satisfactory justification for the sudden, unprecedented rejection of the careful deliberations of the 1916 Board. The writer fears they overreacted to the clamoring of some Members of Congress and others who had been pressing for the restoration of the Walker Medal."

The Veterans Affairs Committee's words about Mary's service, "both as a doctor and feminist," also seemed peculiar to some observers of the issue. Historian Byron Farwell speculated that the army had surrendered to social reformers, writing in *The Washington Times* that "political pressure from women's groups caused it [Mary's medal] to be posthumously restored."

Supporters of the reinstatement outnumbered her critics, however, pointing out that of the 1,522 Medals of Honor awarded for Civil War service, many were for acts that paled in comparison to Mary's service, and that carrying a gun in engagement with the enemy was not a legitimate prerequisite to receive the award. Medals of Honor were, after all, given to Admiral Richard Byrd for "demonstrating that it is possible for aircraft to travel in continuous flight from a now inhabited portion of the earth over the North Pole and return," and to Charles A. Lindbergh for "displaying heroic courage and skill as a navigator, at the risk of his life, by his nonstop flight in his airplane, the 'Spirit of St. Louis,' from New York City to Paris, France, 20–21 May 1927."

Mary Walker's grand-niece, Helen Hay Wilson, told the *Syracuse Herald-American* on May 1, 1977, that she had vague memories as a little girl of the elderly Dr. Mary at her Bunker Hill home. Mrs. Wilson's grandmother (Mary's sister Luna) told young Helen that if Mary had been a man "they wouldn't have dared take her medal away."

On June 12, 1977, two days after President Carter signed the reinstatement bill, Ann Walker remarked, "I have a feeling of sadness that Dr. Mary died sixty years too early to witness the restoration of her medal. It was her misfortune to be one hundred years before her time, although with typical candor, Dr. Mary always remarked, 'It is the times which are behind *me.*'"

ACKNOWLEDGMENTS

The most valuable printed source on Mary Walker's life is the pioneering work by Charles M. Snyder, whose *Dr. Mary Walker:
The Little Lady in Pants* (1962) seems to have had a small, single printing by a subsidy press and is difficult to find in the
used-book market. I'm grateful to Claudia Rivers of the Special Collections Department, University of Texas at El Paso
Library, for loaning me the copy on file there, and greatly in-
debted to Professor Snyder for his path-making research.

Thanks, too, to Syracuse University's E. S. Bird Library Special
Collections Research Center for use of its Mary Edwards
Walker collection of correspondence, photographs, pamphlets,
and documents, and especially for copying the manuscript
of Mary's unpublished "Incidents Connected with the Army."

Other invaluable resources on aspects of Mary Walker's life
and career include the fine monograph *A Woman of Honor*

by Mercedes Graf, and her introductory essay to a recent reprinting of Mary's 1871 book, *Hit;* the booklet by Charles V. Groat, Ph.D., titled *Dr. Mary Walker: A Reader;* and the books by Elizabeth D. Leonard, *All the Daring of the Soldier: Women of the Civil War Armies* and *Yankee Women: Gender Battles in the Civil War.*

Special thanks to Mr. Justin White, historian of the Town of Oswego, New York, and Town Clerk Theresa Cooper for answering my many questions so patiently.

While many people have helped me in the research behind this book, none of them is responsible for any potential errors in it. I've done my best to keep them out, but if any have crept in, they are mine alone.

SOURCES

Baker, Rachel. *The First Woman Doctor: The Story of Elizabeth Blackwell*. Scranton, Pa.: Scholastic Paperbacks, 1999.

Brown, Warren. "Feminist's Medal of Honor at stake," *The Washington Post*, April 13, 1976.

Civil War Society. *Encyclopedia of the Civil War*. New York: Portland House, 1997.

Cooke, Donald E. *For Conspicuous Gallantry*. Maplewood, N.J.: C. S. Hammond, 1966.

Donovan, Frank. *The Medal: The Story of the Medal of Honor*. New York: Dodd, Mead, 1962.

Ebel, Col. Wil (U.S. Army, ret.). "Safeguarding the Medal of Honor," *The Retired Officer Magazine*, July 1977.

Emert, Phyllis R. *Women in the Civil War*. Lowell, Mass.: Discovery Enterprises, 1995.

Farwell, Byron. "The Medal of Honor was not always awarded for 'courage above and beyond' the call of duty," *Military History*, March 1997.

Garrison, Webb. *A Treasury of Civil War Tales*. Nashville: Rutledge Hill Press, 1988.

Gleason, Kerry, Nancy Osborne, and Ed Vermue. "Mary Edwards Walker, M.D.: A Bibliography," Penfield Library Special Collections, SUNY College at Oswego, n.d.

Graf, Mercedes. *A Woman of Honor: Dr. Mary E. Walker and the Civil War*. Gettysburg, Pa.: Thomas Publications, 2001.

Groat, Charles V. *Dr. Mary Walker: A Reader*. Oswego, N.Y.: Oswego Town Historical Society, 1994.

Hall, Marjory. *Quite Contrary: Dr. Mary Edwards Walker*. New York: Funk and Wagnalls, 1970.

Holbrook, Stewart H. *Dreamers of the American Dream*. Garden City, N.Y: Doubleday, 1957.

Leech, Margaret. *Reveille in Washington, 1860–1865*. New York: Harper and Brothers, 1941.

Leonard, Elizabeth D. *All the Daring of the Soldier: Women of the Civil War Armies*. New York: W. W. Norton, 1999.

———. *Yankee Women: Gender Battles in the Civil War*. New York: W. W. Norton, 1994.

Lockwood, Allison. "Pantsuited pioneer of women's lib, Dr. Mary Walker," *Smithsonian Magazine*, March 1977.

Malone, Dumas. *Dictionary of American Biography*. New York: Charles Scribner's Sons, 1936.

McPherson, James. *Battle Cry of Freedom: The Civil War Era*. New York: Oxford University Press, 1988.

Medical and Surgical History of the War of the Rebellion (Vol. 1 of *Medical History*). Washington, D.C.: Government Printing Office, 1879.

Mikaelian, Allen. *Medal of Honor*. New York: Hyperion, 2002.

"Old Castle Thunder, death of Colonel Alexander, who was

superintendent of this prison," *Richmond Dispatch*, March 3, 1895.

Schott, Joseph L. *Above and Beyond*. New York: G. P. Putnam's Sons, 1963.

Sneden, Private Robert Knox. *Eye of the Storm: A Civil War Odyssey*. New York: Free Press, 2000.

Snyder, Charles M. *Dr. Mary Walker: The Little Lady in Pants*. New York: Vantage Press, 1962.

Starr, Paul. *The Social Transformation of American Medicine*. New York: Basic Books, 1982.

Stevens, Bryna. *Frank Thompson: Her Civil War Story*. New York: Macmillan, 1992.

Walker, Mary Edwards. *Hit: Essays on Women's Rights*. Introduction by Mercedes Graf. (Reprint of 1871 edition.) Amherst, N.Y.: Prometheus Books, 2004.

Wells, John Wesley, and Ira M. Rutkow, eds. *An Alphabetical List of Battles of the War of the Rebellion Compiled from the Official Records of the Office of the Adjutant General and Surgeon General*. American Civil War Surgery Series, no. 11. San Francisco: Norman Publishing, 1990.

INDEX

Index

Dale L. Walker (no relation to Mary) is the author of many historical books, biographies, and literary studies, including such Forge titles as *Legends and Lies: Great Mysteries of the American West; The Boys of '98: Theodore Roosevelt and the Rough Riders; Bear Flag Rising: The Conquest of California, 1846; Pacific Destiny; Eldorado: The California Gold Rush; Westward: A Fictional History of the American West;* and *The Calamity Papers.* He is a recipient of four Spur Awards from Western Writers of America and the Owen Wister Award for lifetime contributions to Western history and literature.

Walker, a member of the prestigious Texas Institute of Letters, is general editor of Forge's "American Heroes" series.